Daisy Turnbull

50 RISKS

A guide to building resilience and independence in the first 10 years

TO TAKE WITH YOUR

KIDS

Hardie Grant

BOOKS

Daisy Turnbull is a teacher and director of wellbeing. She has taught at St Catherine's School in Sydney for eight years, and before that taught across school systems, including at a behavioural school working with students with varying challenges. Before going into teaching, she worked in interactive advertising as a producer and in strategy roles. Daisy is an accredited Lifeline crisis support counsellor and regularly volunteers on the crisis support line. She is the mother of two children, and holds a Combined Bachelors degree in Arts/Commerce, a Graduate Diploma of Secondary Teaching, and a Masters of Arts in Theological Studies. She is also an obsessive crocheter and a terrible runner.

TO JACK AND ALICE, WHO MADE ME A MOTHER.
I LOVE SEEING YOU GROW AND BECOME EXCELLENT HUMANS.

Contents

Foreword **6**

Introduction **8**

The first year (for parents) **44**

On the move (1–4) **60**

School days (5–10) **120**

The final risk **194**

Resources **202**

Acknowledgements **204**

'Difficulties strengthen
the mind, as labor
does the body.'

— SENECA

Foreword

The phrase 'no risk, no reward' is based on the idea that taking a chance gives you the only opportunity of receiving the good consequence of a venture. But when children face risks, they get the bonus of four rewards for every challenge attempted:

1. a boost of confidence that their parents have faith in them;
2. discovering that the feeling of fear is often more about a sense of anticipation and not something necessarily to avoid;
3. learning to cope when things don't completely work out;
4. and increased confidence for their *parents* too, which may inspire the parents to encourage the family to take on more challenges – and even take more risks themselves.

As the cherry on top, children receive the potential joy and satisfaction of completing each new activity.

Daisy has written an important and timely book that inspires parents to support their children in taking essential risks – and in age groups where parents can exponentially build children's future confidence and capabilities. With a down-to-earth, practical and humorous approach, combined with nods to science, psychology and *Bluey*, Daisy gives parents a crucial to-do list for their children to slowly face challenges, learn to cope with varied outcomes, and gain more confidence with the accomplishment of each experiment. Most importantly, taking these risks will enhance family wellbeing in time together and time apart, and allow children to discover the wonderful turn life takes when daily activity is not dominated by screens ... or fear of failure.

I'd strongly recommend you and your family take on the challenges (and adventures!) contained within these pages. I'm sure all will enjoy the journey, as well as the results.

DR JUDITH LOCKE
CLINICAL PSYCHOLOGIST

Introduction

It sounds counterintuitive to say that the longer you let kids be kids, the better they will 'adult', but it is true. Research suggests that the more kids are allowed to play in mud, create games, and develop their own solutions to problems, the more they will thrive later in life.

A few years ago I was attending the baptism of a friend's child and the priest asked what kind of person the parents wanted their child to be. I often think about this question and the answers it prompts. We want children to be kind. We want them to have perspective and empathy and compassion: empathy is feeling another person's emotions; compassion has the added element of wanting to help someone without their problems becoming yours. We want our children to be resilient and self-aware. We want them to be resourceful and respectful, and we want them ready to face the world as responsible adults.

But amid all these desires we seem to have fallen into the trap of thinking we are responsible for every single one of our child's positive characteristics, and even more so any negative ones. Millennial kids (like me) and older generations almost certainly didn't have our parents standing next to us with a clipboard and pen checking that we were achieving KPIs. 'Curiosity? Bucketloads. Resilience? Room for improvement.' Instead, they let us learn and develop these skills ourselves.

Parenting has changed in the past forty years. Our expectations of parents have increased incrementally from the 1980s, with the rise of helicopter parenting (overprotective 'hovering' that discourages a child's independence) and mother guilt, not to mention working-mother guilt and stay-at-home-mother guilt. Parenting, especially mothering, has more guilt associated with it than a confessional. And there seems to be a divide in society: on the one side there is this Victorian-era 'children must be seen and not heard' philosophy, where parents bring pre-emptive earbuds for their fellow passengers when they are flying with a baby, and on the other a view that kids should always be able to be kids, and that parents (and other adults) should change their plans to accommodate that. I generally support the latter, but we probably need to find a midpoint – and stop judging parents. Then COVID-19 happened, and parents were shocked by those who either had to or chose to keep sending their kids to day care or school. Running a full day of learning with a child while also working a full-time job became the final frontier of parenting.

Even before corona, parenting had become a lot more risk averse. Helicopter parenting isn't a brand-new concept. Those stories of kids being told to go out and play and come home when the streetlights came on are not the stories of twenty- or even thirty-somethings anymore; they are the stories of their grandparents. We have generations that have been sheltered from risks, and taught to see the world as an inherently risky place. This is not to discount the very real risks the world can pose, especially for children. But measured, limited and monitored risk-taking for children is one pathway to them becoming resilient, confident adults.

'I HAD TO WALK TEN MILES TO SCHOOL, IN THE SNOW!'

We love to remind the next generation of kids how good they have it. I struggle to consider what the equivalent to the above statement is for someone who grew up in the 1980s – we had to wait for our favourite song to come on the radio so we could record it onto a cassette? And it is even harder to think what kids growing up today will have to humble-brag about in their adult years – perhaps only having twenty streaming services to choose from? Clearly, the removal of some childhood risks has been a very welcome and necessary thing – the greater scrutiny around child safety in schools, for example, and more creative and safer play equipment so there are fewer broken bones. But ultimately, society has removed many of the natural risks and opportunities for resilience that previously existed in childhood, so we need to create them.

I am a high school teacher and run the wellbeing program at an independent girls' school in Sydney. I am also the mother to two young kids, Jack and Alice. I often felt like I was learning everything about childhood development, positive psychology and resilience in double time: what I read about or learned in professional development at school could be applied to my home life, and what I practised at home with the kids was often the test run for implementing activities at school. Being a parent gave me more compassion for the difficulties parents experience when dealing with schools, and being a teacher gave me a lot more gratitude for the amazing work Jack's teachers and school community do. (Being both a teacher and a parent also means I get judged no matter which job I'm doing, whether it's telling my kid it's 'their toy, their responsibility' in the playground, or being told by people that 'it must be so great to have all those holidays'.) There has not been a professional development session that I have attended without sending notes to my mum friends.

It was in one of those professional development sessions that I started joking with a friend that what we need is a checklist of risks kids should take before they get to high school, or before they can officially be considered an adult. And that friend thought it was a good idea for a book. I'm not a child psychologist or resilience guru, but I am a mother and a teacher with a strong understanding of wellbeing and positive psychology. I've drawn on my hands-on experience of parenting to write this book, along with my professional experience of teaching teens who come through childhood with radically varying levels of resilience and self-efficacy.

I am not a perfect mother. My children are far from perfect children, and they are still growing up, so I can't tell you what they will be like when they're adults. But I do believe in developing autonomy in the kids and raising them to be kind, curious, and critical thinkers. We want our kids to develop the skills to pick themselves up when they fall, to know when to ask for help and who to ask, but also to be confident that they can solve a lot of their problems themselves. The growing prevalence of mental illness and anxiety among children and teens today tells us just how badly these skills are needed, and the only way to develop them is to let our kids be kids. Let them try, and fall, and fail. Love them and support them, but trust in their resilience, too. They're far more equipped for this journey than we realise.

Risks

This book is titled *50 Risks to Take With Your Kids*, but I want to focus on the three most important words in there, so the next three sections are going to talk about 'risks', 'with' and 'kids'.

Risks and kids generally sound like a rather bad mix. A child's prefrontal cortex, which helps with decision-making and acts as a control centre for our emotions, doesn't fully develop until they're in their twenties (recent research indicates it takes men until they are thirty!). This means that children aren't able to assess risk, control emotions or make decisions in the same way as an adult. I am not a neuroscientist – I can't even draw a brain properly – but my amazing illustrator has attempted one here.

There are two parts of your brain that affect your risk tolerance: your amygdala and your prefrontal cortex. Your amygdala is where you emotionally process everything, and as anyone who has been near a two-(or ten)-year-old knows, it can very easily

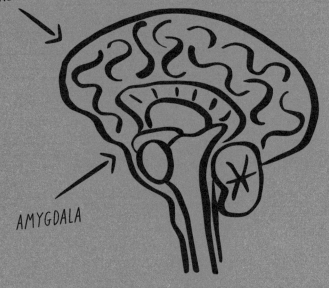

PREFRONTAL CORTEX

AMYGDALA

go into overdrive when you're stressed or upset. If you're emotional and your amygdala is in overdrive, your prefrontal cortex actually shuts down, and you are probably not going to make great decisions.

The relationship between these two parts is important. You might think this means that it's best to limit risks with kids because they are not able to make complex decisions. But careful risk-taking (which sounds like a contradiction in terms, I know) actually allows children to practise managing their emotions and stress when making decisions and acting independently, and gives them the opportunity to build resilience.

Resilience is 'so hot right now'. And so it should be; we are too eager to protect children from life's difficulties, and as a result we ignore their need to develop resilience. Our ability to respond to adversity is like doing push-ups – you will only improve if you practise.

Essayist and statistician Nassim Nicholas Taleb writes that he'd rather be 'dumb and antifragile than smart and fragile'. Taleb considers three categories: fragility, resilience and antifragility. Fragile things break, like a glass when it hits the floor. Resilient things return to their previous state, like a sippy cup when it hits the floor (over and over again). Antifragile things actually become *stronger* as a result of experience – like a person should. The random events that happen to us and how we respond to those events all help instil antifragility. (To be clear, we are talking about everyday, run-of-the-mill life events, not serious trauma.)

But parents – smart and antifragile parents – are misguidedly using their smarts and antifragility to protect their children from the opportunity to make dumb decisions that they can learn from. This means that when those children individuate at around fourteen (when they form a clear sense of self that is separate to their parents and others, which in fact starts from the toddler years but gets more obvious in the teenage ones), they haven't had the chance to develop these skills. And so, we are in this era of people in their twenties and thirties talking about how hard 'adulting' is.

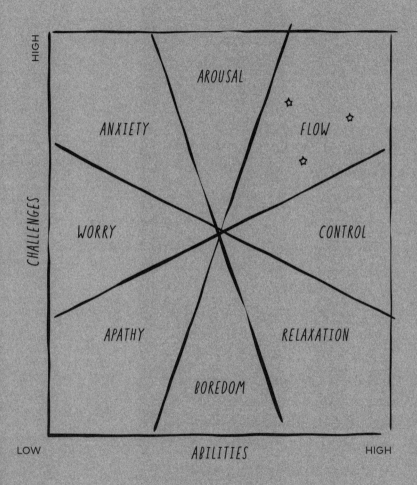

If children are not adequately stimulated in their environment, and are not given the opportunity to take risks, their fear of risk will increase, which can lead to anxiety about exposure to risk. Psychologist Mihaly Csikszentmihalyi (it's pronounced 'chick-sent-me-high') created the theory of flow, which depicts this idea perfectly. Flow is the state you enter when you're slightly challenged by a task that isn't monotonous, and your ability is increasing as you do it. You become focused entirely: think of a one-year-old opening and closing a lift-the-flap book, a two-year-old banging on a drum, a three-year-old looking for rocks in a garden. The state above flow is when the difficulty far outweighs confidence, which can cause anxiety. Conversely, when skill is greater than the difficulty of the task, you get bored. Flow does not end with childhood, it develops throughout our lives. Adults experience flow in their work, in their home lives, and when they're working towards a goal. For children, achieving a state of flow may involve a little bit of risk – like balancing on a wall.

This book is designed to give you some practical suggestions for taking measured risks with your children – risks that have both lived experience and evidence-based research behind them – to develop children who will hopefully turn into good humans and great 'adulters'. There are plenty of brilliant words out there on resilience and child psychology, but I felt we were missing a 'how to', a proactive approach rather than a curative one. And I kept coming back to the idea of taking risks.

These risks are all suggested with the baseline assumption that children are loved, fed and cared for. Some of these risks may not even seem that risky to you, while others may seem totally nuts. These risks are for all parents, but especially the 'overparenter', and can be tailored to suit your child, your family and your circumstances.

A lot of these risks may already occur in many children's lives, so if you are a fairly hands-off parent you may find you are encouraging your children to take some of these steps already. This book will hopefully encourage you to keep pushing yourself and your kids safely out of your comfort zones.

For those parents who struggle a bit more with letting go, this book will help you to help your children find their own autonomy safely. Lenore Skenazy, the author of *Free-range Kids*, refers to a 'worst-first' principle: people think of the worst possible outcome first, especially when it comes to kids. Often you'll think – or people will ask you – 'But what if something terrible happens?' Clearly, that would be terrible. But should one parent based solely on that principle? We don't let tiny probabilities guide our entire lives – otherwise we'd probably never get on a plane or into a car – and we don't want that level of caution to be normalised for our kids either. Without risks, how will kids learn how to live? As that overused Instagram post says, 'Your comfort zone is a beautiful place, but nothing grows there.'

The risks in this book are all designed to develop certain skills, and for that reason they fall into three main categories: physical risks, social risks and character risks. You'll be able to see which particular category each one focuses on by looking for the three key symbols on each page.

PHYSICAL RISKS

Kids are designed to take physical risks, because that is how they learn. Parents are designed to protect their children from physical risks, because that is how kids survive. The trick is getting this balance right.

Exposure reduces fear, and being exposed to physical risks is one of the ways children stop being afraid of everything. Walking for the first time is scary, but the more a child does it, the more competent they become, and the less scary it is. As competence increases, so too does the potential risk involved, but that is a good thing. By keeping your child's risks at a healthy distance above their competency, you will ensure they become more confident and capable.

A 2011 journal article in *Evolutionary Psychology* by two Swedish academics looked at the benefits of 'risky play as a fear reducing behaviour where the child naturally performs exposure behaviour'. One of the issues their research identified is that whenever risk is mentioned in relation to children's play, it doesn't differentiate between minor or severe injuries. Your minor injuries are the ones that can be dealt with at home – bandaids, ice packs, Dettol. Severe injuries require hospitals. But because there are studies that show that 94 per cent of children get injured while climbing a tree, parents assume that climbing trees = serious danger, when actually only around 3 per cent of those injuries were greater than a scrape.

We are currently in a stage where the risks of childhood activity have all been grouped together as equal, and the assumed potential outcome is always severe injury. The physical risks in this book may result in minor injuries. So pack the bandaids, and relax.

SOCIAL RISKS

This second category consists of risks that help children develop the skills that will make them a better friend, family member and colleague. As our lives are being lived online more and more, it can be easy to think that the way we behave in one context doesn't define us in another. But by having a clear set of values, you'll ensure those values are practised across all mediums of your child's life. This could include any of the following characteristics.

SELF-AWARENESS

Self-awareness is at once incredibly simple and very complex to teach. It is partly about being aware of how you are behaving in a conscious way, as opposed to being on autopilot. But it also relates to being aware of who you are in relation to other people.

PERSPECTIVE AND EMPATHY

Everyone will have worked with someone or known someone who can't see a situation from anyone else's point of view. Perspective is a skill that is learned. Social risks can be opportunities for your child to learn how to consider other people's perspectives, and through that feel empathy for them.

RESPECT AND KINDNESS

Some risks will involve children talking to people they may not know. At the least we want them to be respectful in those interactions, but even more than that, we want them to be kind – as a habit, as part of their character.

CHARACTER RISKS

The third category are those character-building risks that help your child develop their internal skills and their ability to deal with life. A lot of this leans on the work of Professor Lea Waters and her theories of strength-based parenting. These risks are about using your child's inner strengths to help them develop identity and character.

RESILIENCE AND REGULATION

You might wonder why resilience is so far down this list given that it's been mentioned approximately seventeen times before now. While all of these risks will build some form of resilience, some are specifically going to focus on it as a character trait. Resilience isn't 'sucking it up' or 'getting over it'. Resilience is about learning and growing from experience. Humans, especially children, can be what Nassim Nicholas Taleb refers to as 'antifragile': not only can we not break, but we can get stronger when faced with difficult situations. The building of strength only happens if we don't let ourselves get too caught up in those difficult situations, which can cause anxiety. This means when we learn about resilience, we are also learning how to regulate ourselves. It is, in fact, a two for one.

RESOURCEFULNESS

Psychologist and author Dr Judith Locke once said that you want your kid to occasionally lie to you, because it shows early problem-solving and resourcefulness skills. The most resourceful kid is the one who, when stealing cookies from a cookie jar, turned the interrogation into a catchy song that passes the blame around the room. There are whole books and articles that discuss the psychological impacts of children lying, but resourcefulness in this book is the ability to recognise a problem, think creatively, and come up with solutions. Spoiler alert – boredom is really good for resourcefulness.

RESPONSIBILITY

What responsibilities should a child have? This is a big question that flummoxes some parents. Giving kids too much responsibility might make you seem like 'the worst parent ever', while too little will not allow them to develop an understanding of their responsibilities as a human. At its heart, teaching children about responsibilities is about consequences. If you are responsible for something and that thing doesn't happen, or doesn't work, there is a consequence. So some of these risks will teach children about how to develop responsibility in an age-appropriate way.

PARENTING RISK

Whether you are reading this as a mother, father, guardian, step-parent, a grandparent wishing your kids would raise your grandchildren the way you raised them, whatever – there are also some specific risks for *you*. They are still focused on developing skills and strengths in your child, but they're a bit more specific to your actions and decisions, rather than to your child's. This book may also provide the opportunity for parents to rethink their relationship with risk at a stage where risk-aversion can always seem like the more 'responsible' choice.

With

These risks are designed to be done *with* your child. It is not fifty things parents have to do, or fifty risks kids should take while their parents are doing other things. These are opportunities to connect and develop your relationship with your child. The activities in the book should hopefully be fun for both you and your kids, and an opportunity for you to bond.

Sure, some of these risks involve letting your kid do something on their own, but you're still the one making that decision. They also give you the chance to talk to your kids about risk, and why some risk is good and too much is bad. Having a child who considers the risks before they hurl themselves down a staircase on a boogie board (hypothetically) is a win.

Hopefully this book will spark a broader conversation between you and your child about risks, how to approach them, and how important our decisions are, so that when the time comes, they can make those decisions and take those calculated risks without you. As your child grows more independent, finding things you can still do together is fundamental to maintaining your connection. This is a great way to pursue those opportunities.

Kids

Seems a bit weird to write a book about kids and not actually talk about kids. What is a kid? A kid is a child, but every child is different, and every year of childhood is wildly different from the last. In the first year it can seem like your baby changes every single day. Then you have to rouse your six-year-old from their slumber one morning and you realise they are basically a teenager. How did that happen?

Childhood is not eighteen years, or ten years, or five. It is a series of developmental stages that are approximately linked to your child's age – although from a parent's perspective some children seem to change overnight.

When my firstborn, Jack, was two and we had moved beyond the Wonder Weeks app (which charts the developmental leaps babies experience in their first twenty months of life), I read about Erik Erikson's life cycle theory. Erikson was a developmental psychologist who coined the phrase 'identity crisis', so we actually quote him all the time. He outlined eight key stages of psychosocial development and saw each stage as having a conflict – one concept against another, which we navigate as we develop. Here I'm going to focus on the first four, as they take in the age range that this book focuses on.

THE FIRST FOUR STAGES OF ERIK ERIKSON'S LIFE CYCLE THEORY

BIRTH–18 MONTHS OLD: TRUST VERSUS MISTRUST

This trust is built on predictability of care: having trust in those around you because they look after you. A lot of this is seen in secure attachment and physical connections with parents and caregivers. If developed properly, it will lead to hope, while an absence of trust can lead to anxiety and fear.

18 MONTHS–3 YEARS OLD:
AUTONOMY VERSUS SHAME

This is when a child develops their sense of will, and for this reason, many of the risks in this book will be focused on this area. When a child is not given the opportunity to practise autonomy, not only will they doubt their own abilities, but they may feel shame about not being able to do things.

3–5 YEARS OLD:
INITIATIVE VERSUS GUILT

Before they start at school, preschoolers need to develop purpose through creating, planning and controlling interactions with other people. This could occur when they invent a simple game of make-believe with friends at preschool. By controlling children during this stage with overly prescriptive activities, they do not develop this initiative and may feel a sense of guilt because they in turn try to be too forceful (overusing the sense of will they developed in the previous stage), which will then lead to punishment. And if you don't treat your child's growing curiosity with respect, they will feel guilty about asking questions.

6–12 YEARS OLD: INDUSTRY VERSUS INFERIORITY

At this stage your child develops their skill of competence. This is when you as a parent need to step back and let your child do the thing, so they learn the skill, so they know they can do harder things. This is where you become a coach rather than the boss, and recognise your child's own ability to develop and grow. This stage, if not practised, can have significant effects on your child's ability, confidence and self-esteem, which are all really important when they start high school.

At all of these stages, encouraging your child to take risks is going to help them to maintain that trust, that autonomy, that initiative and that industry.

These stages need to be recognised as your child experiences them, because each is the foundation of the next, and it is so much harder to develop hope, will, purpose or competence from scratch as a teenager. As a teacher, I have seen many cohorts of students finish school, and the observation I've made is that the students who thrive, who are leaders, who excel at sport or music or debating, or who are just really kind humans, are those with parents who have developed their own child's competence, and done so steadily, since they were young.

AN EDUCATIONAL APPROACH TO PARENTING: BACKWARDS MAPPING

There's a key strategy in teaching used by curriculum writers, departments and individual teachers that's known as backwards mapping. In other words, you start with where you want the student to end. What do you want a student who has studied history for thirteen years to be able to do? What does that mean you want them to be able to do at the end of Year 10? Year 8? Year 7? Once you've identified the end goal, all learning can be designed as steps to get the student closer to that point.

Parenting should be the same. We don't know what our kids will be like – their personalities come out on their own and in their own time – but by having an idea of what skills we want them to have when they are teenagers, or adults, we can start working towards that goal as they grow up.

It can be very easy to get stuck on the hamster wheel of daily life. As a friend of mine says, 'The days are long but the weeks are short' (okay, so it turns out my friend stole it from Gretchen Rubin). I think even the weeks can be long too, and in the midst of it all we can forget the kind of children we hope to raise, and end up filling in the gaps later on, rather than building up their strengths as our kids grow.

This book is focused on children up to the age of ten. That is because a lot of the skills I'm talking about need to be developed before your child is a teenager so that they have the ability to recognise the difference between a 'good risk' and a 'risky risk'. Teenagers are aware of the potential negative outcomes of a risk, but they will usually focus on the potential positive outcomes instead, thanks to that pesky underdeveloped prefrontal cortex. By bringing your child up with an understanding of and preparation for risks in life, they will be more skilled in risk assessment and risk calculation by the time they hit the crucial teenage years.

The fifty risks here are arranged into a general ascending order by age, with the majority in the five-to-ten-year-old bracket, because that is when kids are most likely to start doing things on their own, as their competency and desire for independence grows. This book isn't designed to be read cover to cover (although you're welcome to do that). Dip in and out of the relevant risks for your child at their age, and revisit the book a month or a year or two later, to explore new risks. You may find that some involve getting your child to do things a bit earlier than you'd expected – go with it! You'll really find out what they're capable of.

Remember, this is not something that you do as some kind of parenting High Intensity Interval Training; it's something that's built on over years. It's also not something you need to constantly do, but you do need to consciously do it, when you can. The more you do it, the more it will become part of your everyday parenting.

These risks are part of the steps you could take to raise children who are confident, autonomous, compassionate and responsible. I hope you walk away from this book with sensible and practical strategies to help your kids be the excellent humans you want them to be.

'The job of a parent
is to work yourself
out of a job.'

— JONATHAN HAIDT

The first year

(FOR PARENTS)

The months before your baby can crawl and walk are the cuddliest, but also the scariest, because it feels like it is all on you. For this stage, I haven't suggested any risks for your child to take because it's already a very personal and varying time. Instead I have included a number of parenting risks. These offer some ways of thinking that could be different to what you read online or in parenting books (although I have also included the parenting books that I loved when going through this stage with Jack and Alice in my resources on pages 202–203).

1. Remember, they can't fall off the floor

When your child is a baby, before they are crawling or walking, it can be hard to keep from watching them like a hawk. This is partly because they are very cute and make amazing noises, and you just want to be near them all the time. But the first 'risk' you can expose your child to is as much for you as it is for them. Lay them on a blanket or towel on the floor, somewhere they can't fall off. Make sure there aren't any dangerous things around them, like pieces of LEGO or enriched uranium, and then step away. Not for ages, but maybe a few minutes. A great place to practise this risk is on a bath mat while you have a shower. (My friend did this once and her baby had the best nap he'd had in weeks.)

Now this might seem like the lamest of risks, but it is doing two things. One, it is giving you time to yourself, in short bursts, which is important for avoiding parental burnout. Secondly, it is showing your child that they can actually spend a few minutes on their own. If you want evidence that this works, look at the experience between firstborns, who often get more attention than they know what to do with, and subsequent children who are often left to their own devices while their older siblings are demanding something.

While I do love academic research, I am instead about to illustrate this theory with a quote from Seth Meyers' stand-up show *Lobby Baby*.

'I'm fascinated by the youngest of three kids. They're so much more interesting than the other kids. They're so resourceful and self-reliant because they've received so much less attention in their lives ... You know, when you have one two-year-old, they're crying for you to make a smoothie. When your third is two years old, they make the smoothie. They just walk into the kitchen, drag in a stool, get up on top of it, start throwing bananas into a blender. And it's not even your blender. It's a blender they bought from a job they have on the side.'

– SETH MEYERS

PARENTING RISK

$2.$ Add a baby to your routine (not always the other way around)

I remember when I started going to mothers' group, there was one mum who always came with her make-up done. I was amazed. How did she manage make-up when I was barely managing to wear pants? But what I quickly realised is that in those first few crazy months, we all have one thing we will not give up. Hers was make-up. Mine was coffee.

I have a friend who didn't ever want to go to a cafe because her baby might cry. Babies cry. Some babies cry a lot, and some babies don't. But crying babies are a part of the first year of parenting, and if you trap yourself at home in the

cycle of sofa–change table–bed–sofa–change table–bed, you won't develop your own skills to get out of the house with a baby, which will make the next few years even harder. Because if a crying baby scares you, just wait until they're a rampaging toddler.

So if you have something you love to do, and you're worried about doing it with a baby, don't be. Find a way to add your baby to that routine. Whether it is getting out of the house for half an hour, cooking something that isn't pureed, going to the gym, whatever. Try to do it. It will be really hard the first few times, but stick with it. The risk will pay off for your own sense of achievement, autonomy and enjoyment of being a parent.

3. Leave the baby (with a responsible adult)

Whether you are the mother, father, guardian or whatever, it can be very scary to leave a baby with someone else. Especially when there are boobs and breastfeeding involved. But I would suggest that doing this, even once, even for an hour, in the first six months of being a parent, would be a risk you can handle, and one that will help everyone involved grow.

At around the age of six to nine months, babies learn that in fact they are not the same person as their primary parent. At this stage, leaving the baby with a new person is difficult. If that person has been left with the baby before, it is not nearly

as difficult. The point is, you're going to have to do it at some point, so do it earlier.

When Jack was around three months old, we planned to go for dinner and my parents offered to babysit. The milk was expressed, the breast pads were in, the baby was handed over to my mum, and my dad finally thought he had a chance of being able to hold Jack. We went to a restaurant approximately five minutes away. We spent the whole dinner worrying about the baby and returned about an hour later. But the baby was asleep. The baby survived. We survived. The grandparents remain integral to our kids' lives.

To this end, I would also suggest leaving the baby with the other parent as often as possible. Annabel Crabb talks about this as a societal issue in her book *The Wife Drought* and the *Quarterly Essay* 'Men at Work'. The reason this is so important to do in the first year is that you can very easily get into the situation Crabb describes as the 'casual implied assumption that my partner is a simpleton who cannot make a Vegemite sandwich unsupervised'. That is a learned response of women (for the most part) who have fallen into the habit of getting jobs done themselves because it is easier than watching their (for the most part) male partner struggle with figuring it out. The 'mere male' concept might have made sense forty years ago, but it shouldn't anymore. Also, couples who share chores more have more sex, so that's another good reason to make sure both parents are actively looking after the kids.

4. Forget about all the judgement

I think if we were to consider the jobs that are most often and thoughtlessly judged by society, they would be those of parents, especially mothers, and teachers (trust me, I know). The latter are judged because almost everyone has spent thirteen years in a classroom and is therefore an expert in teaching. And parents are judged because everyone has had a parent, or is a parent, or knows a parent.

Parenting has changed a lot between the generations, and will continue to do so. Forty years ago there were no baby monitors, let alone heart

rate monitors built into cots, and there was no expectation that parental involvement in children's education would go beyond reading school report cards. Every generation thinks they had it or did it best. Every couple without kids knows exactly how they would parent – with no screens, no sugar, and no sense of reality.

As a parent, you will be judged. You are going to be judged by people who have never met you, by people who see you on the bus, who watch you at the supermarket.

I am a brave person. I once had a man in his sixties give me a look when I was breastfeeding Jack in a cafe. I said, 'His taxes are going to pay for your pension so you'd better hope he's well nourished.' The guy jumped out of his skin so quickly that I worried my tax dollars were going to pay for his trip to the cardiology ward.

That line did not come to me out of nowhere – he wasn't the first person to cast a disapproving look in my direction. It's good to have a comeback. Generally the comeback will lead to the judgy bear saying something lovely like, 'I was just admiring how well you were doing considering X,' or, 'I don't know how you guys do it these days, it wasn't this complicated when I was young.' But beyond having comebacks, which are admittedly pretty superficial, have the confidence in your own parenting to know that a judgy look from a stranger isn't going to make you doubt yourself. Backing yourself is the greatest comeback you can have. And make sure, when you're not in the trenches of parenting, that you don't judge those who are.

'When I was a kid, we used to get up in the morning at half past ten at night, half an hour before we went to bed, eat a lump of poison, work twenty-nine hours a day at mill for your lifetime ... You try to tell that to the young people of today, will they believe you?'

— THE FOUR YORKSHIREMEN

On the move

(1-4)

There are moments of fog lifting as your baby graduates to being a toddler. They happen slowly, and don't last very long. You look up and realise that while you've been scrolling Instagram for ten minutes, your nine-month-old was repeatedly putting a toy through a toilet roll tunnel. You wake up realising you haven't been woken up (maybe this happens in the first year, maybe it doesn't). But gradually, the fog really does start to lift. This is when you can enjoy the fun of small people with their own personalities. As they grow, this is a great time to embrace some risks that encourage more independence.

5. Roam free

When parents in the 50s or even the 90s had children, they would keep the baby in a play pen because it was safe and contained. The rest of the house was a grown-up fantasy of vases on shelves and cupboard doors that opened with ease. Now, however, parents seem to be babyproofing the entire house and letting kids colonise every nook and cranny with pieces of DUPLO and sucked-on toast.

Some children are obsessed with getting into locked cupboards, but if your child isn't, then you don't need to lock every cupboard. Giving children the opportunity to explore without constraint will teach them more about their own safety and awareness than making sure they never get into that cupboard. Obviously electricity and power points are dangerous, but don't keep safety locks on for longer than you need to. I would suggest

a defensive protection of your house rather than offensive – protect as needed, rather than pre-emptively. The only people telling you that you must have every single thing babyproofed are the makers of babyproofing products. I say this as someone who still has safety locks on the kitchen drawers that her six-year-old knows how to open, and that I don't know how to remove.

Also, remember to let your baby have some free-range fun, where they can explore and discover without being unsafe, perhaps in the backyard or a playground.

6. Eat sand, sniff dirt, get sick

Kids eat dirt. My daughter can make herself a three-course meal out of sand. As parents, we worry about germs, especially when our children are coming out of the newborn stage and entering the 'if I can pick it up, it's going in my mouth' stage.

I am not going to tell you when you can stop sterilising bottles and dummies because I am *not* a doctor, but the 'hygiene hypothesis' argues that some exposure to microbes helps develop a child's immune system. Luckily, finding these germs isn't hard – they are in playgrounds, parks, beaches and the garden. Germs, for the most part, live outside.

In the book *Dirt Is Good*, doctors Jack Gilbert, Rob Knight and Sandra Blakeslee showed that in our desire to protect our children from disease in the short term (fewer colds and gut issues), we have weakened their immunity to other diseases like asthma and eczema. A Swedish study even showed that children whose parents 'suck' their child's dummy to make it clean (which of course, it doesn't), had fewer rates of asthma as they grew up. Other research shows that owning a dog (see risk 39) during pregnancy also increases your child's immunity and decreases their risk of obesity – and not just because they want to chase the dog around the place!

There is another reason for embracing germ exposure. I went back to work when Jack was eight months old, and Jack went to day care. During that time I had to take heaps of sick days because Jack constantly got sick, but a girlfriend reassured me that kids who go to day care before school have far fewer sick days once they do start school. My wonderful friend wasn't just trying to make me feel better – actual evidence backs her up. The more colds and tummy bugs and sniffles your child gets before they are two and a half, the fewer they should get as they get older. So more sick days in day care means fewer sick days at school. Jack is a testament to that: he only had one day off in his whole first year of school.

Washing hands and safe food preparation are important, of course, but don't freak out about the germs that your kids could encounter outside or at day care. Instead, remember that they are developing their immune systems by doing kid things.

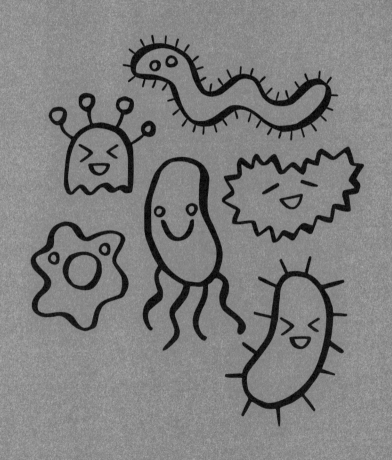

7. Help-not-help

There is nothing quite as unhelpful as a helpful toddler. Hours of productivity have been wasted allowing toddlers to help-not-help cut vegetables, or fold laundry. A two-year-old is not going to be able to put their laundry away. A three-year-old is probably not going to put it away properly. A four-year-old might, and a five-year-old absolutely should be able to. But, as with many things in life, we can only put our laundry away properly if we've had the opportunity to do it badly multiple times previously.

It is tempting to distract your kids with TV so you can have a moment to put away the laundry, or pack away the shopping, but sometimes it is better to let your child help-not-help, even when you just want to get the job done. A child who is helping-not-helping is learning how to actually help, and they will eventually get better at it. They are seeing the jobs their parents do around the house, and letting them get involved means they won't feel as though they are entitled to not do those jobs.

Start with small tasks, and focus on consistency over perfectionism. Eventually, give them their own list of jobs. Mix it up between individual jobs (cleaning their lunch box) and family jobs (tidying the living room), so it's clear that they are not only responsible for themselves, they are also a part of a family unit. Sure, each job might take twice as long to do at first, but eventually, you may not have to do the job at all. And bonus – you have raised a child who understands the importance of people helping each other.

PARENTING RISK

8. Consciously sit on LEGO

It's natural to want to leave kids who are playing to their own devices, or *on* their own devices. But it is important to take opportunities to consciously connect with your kids when you can, even if it is just for a quarter of an hour. The decision to put your phone away or leave the dishes in the sink in order to play a game of UNO or do some drawing is a risk, because it is counter to how we live our lives – in a flurry of multitasking.

This probably sounds like it is in conflict with many of the risks in this book, which focus on getting your children to be more independent. But independence starts with connection. Jennifer Kolari, a family therapist who founded *Connected Parenting*, writes about the importance of having

consciously connected time with your kids. Kolari's research has shown that fifteen minutes of one-on-one time with your kid of an evening, doing what they want – whether that's playing with soft toys or having a dance off or reading the same book for the eleventy billionth time – can make bedtime easier. This is because some kids, especially when they are young and in day care, can feel that going to bed is another big separation from their parents. That can seem scary. Dedicating that time to your child can give them a release of oxytocin that will develop their emotional security and their ability to develop healthy connections with others.

We can't always be 100 per cent focused on our kids – and frankly, doing so would be disastrous – but making time to consciously sit on LEGO or get covered in glitter with your child will give them the secure attachment they need to become more independent when they're older.

9. Play with sticks

Playgrounds are wonderful at developing certain skills – how to go down a slide, scramble up a rope and take turns – but there is also something to be said for less structured play, either in nature or at home, that involves building the space as much as playing in it. The creation of an imaginary world through arranging sticks or rocks or even lines in sand develops imagination as well as physical strength.

While there has been a shift to more open-minded play spaces, most playgrounds are still very prescriptive (it is a pirate ship, that is all it can be), and the thought of heaving large sticks and rocks around the play area would send most municipal

council workers into cardiac arrest. But children can build forts in spaces that aren't official play areas – parks with bush areas will have sticks, bark and leaves to build with.

Building a fort is basically the kid version of being a management consultant. They see a problem (the lack of a fort) and have to find a way to fix the problem (build a fort) with whatever they have around them (resources), which is a bit like having a budget to deal with. They have to manage their team (you and any other kids who are around) as well as other stakeholders (ensure smaller kids who want to destroy the fort are out of the way).

Forts – or cubbies or rafts or rockets – can also be built at home, and require a huge amount of mess, as well as patience from parents. Leave the fort up for the whole weekend – so long as that doesn't mean you have to sleep without a pillow. Let your kid enjoy their achievement.

Building a fort can also be about being present for your kid. Let them lead the activity, and even if you can see that the pillow or stick clearly needs to go behind the wall to keep it structurally sound, don't say so. Let your child figure it out. Ask questions like, 'What do you think we should do with this sheet?' or, 'I wonder where this could go to keep the flux capacitor secure?' Once you see your child entering that state of 'flow', try to step away and let them work on their own, until they ask for help. You might be needed actively, or they may want you to be less involved but still supporting them.

10. Climb a tree

Tree climbing is a bit of a lost art. Many people don't have a big tree in their backyard, and most playgrounds are focused on equipment rather than nature. However, tree climbing has been shown to have both physical and cognitive benefits, helping children develop coordination and strength as well as confidence and problem-solving skills.

So take your kids to a park that has some big trees (with accessible first branches) and let them try climbing. Try not to help them – let them figure it out themselves. The process of working out which branches they can and can't reach is a chance for them to learn about their own limitations and their risk profile. You might feel the need to hover around like a clown with a trampoline the first few times, but just remember, we are descended from apes, and they're pretty good in trees.

Climbing trees is also about being in nature. Bugs can be watched; leaves and flowers can be collected. Spending time in nature gives your children a greater understanding of their world, and the effects we have on it. Nature play also improves fitness and motor skills, and provides greater open-ended ways for children to develop their imaginations. There are nature-based kindergartens opening all over the world, recreating what used to be a standard in many childhoods. You don't need to enrol your kid in a nature-based play activity though, you just need to get them comfortable being outside – and perhaps up a tree.

11. Be bored

Okay, this isn't so much a risk to your child as it is a risk to the state of your home and your sanity. We need to let children be bored. The ability to entertain oneself is learned, and needs to be practised. Technology, weekend sports, birthday parties and generally overbooked schedules mean that this skill is practised less and less frequently. But boredom is important.

Many people believe that 'boredom is for the bored', and that being in a state of boredom demonstrates a lack of creativity or initiative, but in fact boredom is for creative people. Creativity doesn't grow in the over-occupied, it grows in those who have time to let ideas develop, argues Professor Lea Waters, author of *The Strength Switch*. Boredom also develops resourcefulness. Giving your kids a few hours to entertain themselves will develop their ability to find things they want to do with their spare time.

So don't feel guilty if there are some afternoons where you have no plans. Having no plans can be the very thing your kid needs to come up with the best ideas. When you notice your child playing on their own, leave them. If they ask to watch TV, try to delay it. I find that asking Jack to put his shoes away when he comes home generally leads to 20 minutes or so of him playing happily on his own. Set up some toys with your child, then tell them you need to go and do something else. In the short term you might hear 'I'm bored' ad nauseam, and your home will get really messy, but eventually, you'll think your child has run away and you'll freak out, only to discover they're in their room playing LEGO silently and didn't hear you call their name five times . Hypothetically.

12. Make friends with adults

When your child is no longer an attached infant, it can still feel risky to 'hand them over' to another adult, even when that adult is someone you know well. Without considering any actual dangers, what if your kid blurts out something embarrassing about your own life? Kids have no filter – Alice once shared with everyone at day care that I 'got in trouble at work for knitting' (I didn't).

For all the talk we have about it taking a 'village' to raise a child, we don't seem to rely on others as often as we should. Whether it is a grandparent, an aunty, a godparent, a nanny or a day care educator, it is incredibly important for children to develop strong emotional relationships with charismatic adults who are not their parents, who they can talk to openly and frankly about anything, including when

they think you are being unfair. Parenting author Maggie Dent refers to these people as 'lighthouses', and family psychologist Dr Michael Carr-Gregg argues that having another adult in a child's life is a key factor in them growing up to be a resilient adult.

These days it's rare to find multiple generations living under the same roof, or even in the same city, and there is a tendency to socialise with other families so the kids can hang out with other kids. That means these relationships often need to be sought out rather than stumbled upon. So, when you notice that your child has a favourite aunty, or clicks with a family friend who you trust, nurture that relationship by inviting them around, or asking them to take your child to the park. Encourage phone conversations and FaceTime with them. Later on, especially in the teenage years, that adult will be a great source of wisdom and perspective.

13. Get out of routine (sometimes)

Apparently Barack Obama wore the same white shirt every day in the White House so he didn't have to make any more decisions before, you know, running the country. Routines keep us from having to reinvent the wheel every day, and are hugely important for young kids, especially around things like bath and bedtimes. However, there is something to be said for occasionally stepping out of our routines and seeing what happens.

The time this happens most naturally is during holidays, whether it be a staycation over a long weekend or going on a family trip. Holidays, no matter how near or far, how budget or glamorous, provide great opportunities for kids of any age (and adults) to learn. Travel can expose us to risks that we wouldn't otherwise get a chance to take. Plus, they are times for families to bond. Holidays create memories, and positive family memories are important in helping protect a child's resilience and sense of self as they become adults.

We went on a holiday with our kids when they were almost four and almost one, and I was amazed at how much Jack in particular grew up during our two weeks away. Working-mother guilt swept over me: did that mean he'd be a higher functioning human if I was at home with him all the time? But in fact, it was from a change in the day-to-day routine that the growth occurred.

Holidays aren't just about spending more time together. They're also about doing less each day, unless you're on an *Amazing Race*–style adventure. They give you space and time to practise risks with your kids that you may not have the capacity to during your normal routines. Let your children make their own fun while you take some quiet time to nap or read a book (it's your holiday too). Let them scramble up and down rocks at a beach. Watch them, but don't shadow them. Give them opportunities to try doing things on their own, without the pressures of getting to school and work: putting on their own sunscreen and packing their own snacks. These are skills they can use when they get home as well.

But that is not to say that you can't find the opportunity to experience 'holidays' in the everyday by mixing things up a little bit. Professor Ian Hickie talks about the importance of new experiences on a child's brain development – he says 'every new sight, every new sound, every new smell causes the brain to rapidly develop synaptic connections, that is connections between the brain cells, to capture that experience'. Board games, bike rides and little family adventures are all ways to encounter those new experiences and create new memories together. Take the time to slow down.

14. Raid the fridge

You may not consider making a cheese sandwich to be one of the riskiest things you can do, but trust me, when it's a child making that sandwich, the mess is real – at least the first few times. As with all things, the better your child gets at it, the less mess there is, and the less you have to do. Eventually, if you have more than one child, the first child will make snacks for ALL YOUR CHILDREN and you can go and have a nice lie-down.

In case you haven't already figured this out, kids need to snack – a lot. Letting them get their own

snacks will make their constant hunger easier for both you and for them. Firstly, have healthy snacks available. (If your house is full of potato chips and chocolate bars then your kid will eat potato chips and chocolate bars.) Have snacks that your child can open and easily reach; a fruit bowl is great. Cereal is an easy one as well – getting them to make their own breakfast is a huge win. Drinks can be tricky for young kids, but practise pouring with water outside on a hot day: it's fun and won't cause any dramas. And remember, spills are all part of the learning process.

Make sure your child checks that they can have a snack before they get one. A six-year-old who eats a sandwich twenty minutes before dinner isn't likely to eat much dinner, and they need to learn that mealtimes aren't just about eating whenever they want. Fortunately, there's usually someone in our kitchen half an hour or so before dinner, so there's little chance of the kids sneaking a pre-dinner snack. If they do manage this, I'll be calling the early recruitment line for spy agencies.

Making snacks can easily transition into making kindergarten or school lunches too. It is very hard for a child to complain about their lunch when they made it themselves. From the first term of school, Jack started packing his own lunch, with a bit of quality control from us. Every morning he makes a sandwich, gets a muffin that we made a few weeks ago from the freezer, grabs a yoghurt pack, and I try to chuck in an homage to vegetables -- cucumber, corn or carrot. Done. But this wouldn't be the case if he hadn't started getting his own snacks when he was younger, so for the love of autonomy and giving yourself a break, start now!

15. Order their own babycino

My family and I regularly go to a cafe just around the corner from my house. When Jack was around two we started telling him that if he wanted a babycino or something, he had to ask the staff politely for it. We are now almost at the point of letting him go up the road to get coffees – we just need to figure out how to balance KeepCups on his bike!

The skill of talking to a stranger who also has an inbuilt level of societal trust is one that can be nurtured from very early on. Start when the cafe isn't super busy, and accompany your child to the counter if needed. Remind them of the importance of using their manners and speaking clearly when ordering.

Cafes and restaurants also allow opportunities for children to develop their ability to identify people who make them feel uncomfortable. I have seen parents take their ten-year-olds into the bathroom at a cafe even though it is right near their table. Hovering around children all the time outsources that skill to the hoverer, and can have two dangerous potential results – the child not learning to recognise when they feel unsafe, and the child becoming fearful of everyone. This is particularly important given the current disconnect between online and offline safety with the rise of things like social media–connected gaming. Teaching your child to understand their own safety before they're online will make it a lot easier to grasp in a cyber safety context.

So talk to your child about stranger danger and trusted adults, and let them go to the bathroom on their own. And while your child is in the bathroom, steal some of their food, because there's no way they'll share if you ask.

16. Go hungry

My son hates chocolate. It seems that at almost every birthday party there is a chocolate cake. When he was two, I would bring a vanilla cupcake to each party just in case (and eat it on the way home if the birthday cake wasn't chocolate). As he grew up, I realised that I was indulging his own food jag. It is normal to go to another person's party and not like something they have served, and it is weird to bring your own version of that meal. So we had a conversation explaining that if the birthday cake is chocolate, he can just have extra sweets or chips. The only birthday cake he can control is his own.

Some kids do have very specific food jags, and will not eat anything unless it is covered in tomato sauce or cut up into star shapes, for example. But the more kids are faced with the experience of NOT having those jags met, the more prepared they are to face difficulties. Accommodating their every quirk doesn't teach them to compromise, it teaches them that they're entitled to have everything their way, and the world just doesn't work like that. If your kid doesn't like what you've cooked for dinner, resist the urge to get them something else. Don't perpetuate the idea that you're running a restaurant. As my mother always says, 'No child has ever voluntarily starved to death.'

17. Fall off a bike, skateboard or scooter

Sometime before your child is three they get sick of being trapped in the pram, but they're still too small to walk meaningful distances. There is a definite benefit to teaching your child to ride some form of transport – whether it's a bike, a scooter, a skateboard or a hovercraft – before they hit the point where they refuse to go in the pram. You may think that your eighteen-month-old or two-year-old is too young to learn to ride a scooter, but younger siblings are proof that kids can figure this stuff out themselves – usually about six months before you even imagined you'd want them to.

There are a lot of schools of thought on how to learn to ride a bike, including an anti-training wheels theory where kids start on balance or 'strider' bikes, which have no pedals, and learn to balance while moving before graduating to a normal bike. Or there is the way every kid until 2010 learned to ride a bike, with training wheels. Whatever works for your family is the way to go.

Your kid will fall off. Probably several times. The key is to make sure they get back on. Any damage they do to themselves is likely to be minimal, and will be far outweighed by the confidence they'll gain (and the increased mobility you'll both enjoy because you won't have to carry them everywhere).

Be aware of the laws and regulations regarding where kids are allowed to ride, and who with. And make sure your children learn about road safety way before they are old enough to ride anywhere on their own. If you have two or more children, for example, you will inevitably encounter a situation where the eldest has scootered up ahead, and the younger one has a tantrum because her shoes are on the right feet, when she wanted them on the wrong feet, even though she put them on the right feet. And you want that older child to stop at the corner, to wait, and to know what it means to be careful.

18. Come last (or at least second)

Dr Michael Carr-Gregg talks about 'resilience deficit disorder' in kids. Many children are either not playing games at home or at schools because we don't want them to be upset by losing, or they are playing games in such a way that 'everyone wins'.

The greatest opportunity for developing skills at any game is by losing. Humans learn from bad experiences, so play games with your children and allow them to lose sometimes. Maybe not every game – you don't want your child to be perpetually

smashed, but you don't want them to win every single game, either. If they are upset about losing, let them calm down and then talk to them gently about it being a game. You may even want to tell them you will sometimes let them win, and other times you win, so their expectation isn't just that adults are terrible at board games. Until one day, your kid will actually beat you at a board game and you will have to harness your own resilience.

Games like draughts, go fish, UNO or chess are excellent for developing resilience and empathy. There is also the opportunity to practise this with peer-based games like pass the parcel or hide and seek. The more your child is used to the risk of losing, the better they will handle disappointment as they grow up.

PARENTING RISK

19. Let them level up in their own time

During this period between ages one to five, it can be very easy to see your child do something for themselves, like climb up on their highchair, but still continue lifting them into it afterwards. This will be for two main reasons. Firstly, you are on autodrive because your mind is running like a web browser with twenty-three tabs open, and you forget that they can actually do it for themselves now. The second reason is that it is easier/faster/less stressful to just keep doing the thing. But as Lenore Skenazy, founder of the free-range kids movement, says, 'The more you help them, the less you help them.'

Imagine if you were given a promotion at work, and the person whose job you are meant to now have just kept doing the job themselves, right in front of you. It would be incredibly awkward, as well as making you feel a bit useless. So if your small person is learning a new skill, like putting on their shoes, keep giving them the opportunity to practise it. It may (okay, it will) mean everything takes five times longer, and sometimes you just cannot wait, but in general, try to nurture that process.

This all relates to the self-determination theory by professors Richard Ryan and Edward Deci: you want the child to feel a bit challenged by a task while being competent enough to achieve it, and you want them to have autonomy. Autonomy relates to the idea of being independent and intrinsically motivated – they want to learn how to do something for themselves, or for the benefit of the activity itself. But don't feel too much despair at your child having outgrown your help, because the key third element of self-determination theory is relatedness – children need to know they have a loving parent who is there to help them if needed, and who will let them learn at their own pace.

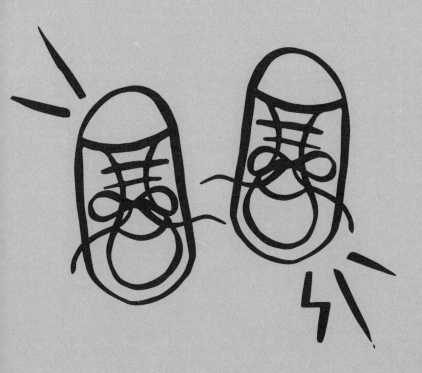

20. **Get really exhausted**

Have you ever looked at photos of families out on hikes and thought, there is no way my child would do that? Think again. The experience of going on a hike or ride is a new adventure for kids, and one that they will love. It's got bugs, it's got sticks, it's got dirt, it's got a picnic at the end of it. What's not to love?

It can seem very daunting to take young kids out for anything longer than a trip to the playground. The equipment, the nappy bag, the change of clothes, water bottles – why bother? Especially given the extremely high chance that you will only get 200 metres from your home before someone needs to go to the toilet. But, despite the effort and the risk of forgetting something, it is worth it.

A friend of mine had his kids riding motocross from age nine, because that's what he loves doing. Regardless of whether you're BMX banditing or just going for walks, there is a great benefit to being in nature. The Japanese call it *shinrin-yoku* – forest bathing. This art of spending time in nature has been known to increase life expectancy and mental wellbeing. So making a habit of going out and spending time in nature as a child will mean this gets added to the arsenal of ways your child can protect themselves against stressful situations when they are adults.

Hikes and bike riding also make for a great family 'thing' to do together. Having a family 'thing' before your kids are teenagers makes it easier to continue it, and saves you scrambling for a ritual once they start to seriously individuate at around thirteen or fifteen. Creating them after that point could prompt a lot of eye rolls. We decided bike riding would be our thing, and so we started with baby steps when the kids were very young – riding to the local cafe, to the local park. It gets us out of the house on a weekend, and is teaching the kids about road safety, directions and, of course, getting back on your bike when you fall off. It is also not just child-centred. Going to playgrounds is great, but that's really for the kids. Getting into the habit of doing activities that the whole family enjoys breaks the idea that every weekend activity needs to be about the kids. Parents need weekends too.

Also – these adventures give you great opportunities for discussion. Walking, riding or even driving, for that matter, are great times for conversations. With a child, there is a power dynamic when you're sitting across the kitchen table talking to each other. This is minimised when you're moving in the same direction. Plus, there is not as much need for eye contact, so the conversation can flow better. So get moving, scrape your knee and have a chat along the way.

21. Clean up their own mess

Depending on how you introduce it, making your child tidy their own room can either be in no way risky, or incredibly stressful. As with most risks, I suggest starting this very early and very small. As soon as your child is walking they can put things in places – toys in a toy box, shoes in a drawer. Starting each day with a routine of pyjamas under the pillow or in the laundry basket will create a habit of putting things away. This habit means cleaning their space will become a much easier task each time.

Kay Wills Wyma wrote a book about her one-year journey getting her five kids, aged three to sixteen, to clean the house. She wrote that picking up socks and towels around the house was not just 'solidifying my children's expectation that someone will always be around to do their work for them' but also that it didn't give them a chance 'to organise their closets based on their own logic'. By getting your kids to be more responsible for their own belongings, you are helping develop both their independence and their sense of organisation – and reducing the chances that they will lose stuff!

It is okay to whinge about having to do household chores. I whine about doing laundry all the time. Doesn't mean I don't do it. It is unrealistic to expect that kids won't complain about having to do a job. Complaining is fine – so long as they know that it won't get them out of doing it.

22. Have the tantrum

I want you to remember a time when you got really annoyed by something that was pretty innocuous. Mine was the printer. I had prepared a whole bunch of past exam papers for students, I hit 'print and delete' on the school's printer system and then it jammed and I'm pretty certain those exam papers flew off into the hyperverse, never to be seen again. I was so annoyed. I growled. Like, actually growled – this visceral throat growl. I tightened my fists, and if I had been any angrier I probably would have smacked the printer. Then I fixed the jam, went back to my office and reprinted the papers.

The fact is, we all have our moments. Big emotions are part of life. And in small kids we call them tantrums. In response to these tantrums, we tend to launch into problem-solving mode, frantic to get our child to calm down. When we do this, we're denying them the opportunity to feel their feelings. This risk is about sometimes letting your child have that tantrum, hearing them, and telling them that it will be okay. Often we can't have the tantrum we want to have – we have to go to that thing, we have to be polite to that person. Explain that to them. But occasionally, let them experience big emotions fully.

This is not about giving them what they want, or distracting them with screen time or ice cream or a toy. In fact, it is really important that you don't let your child think a tantrum will be rewarded in any way. Just talk to them. Tell them you love them, that you're there for them when they need you, and let them go.

Kids need to know they can be vulnerable. Professor Brené Brown talks about the importance of avoiding shame when kids are experiencing big emotions. Brown explains that what we are and what we do teaches children far more than what we try to teach them – so 'we must be what we want our children to become'. If you want your child to be able to be honest about their emotions, you need to model this by being honest about your own.

There is also something to be said for the language of emotions. 'Sad' can refer to a multitude of emotions; so can 'angry'. Teach your children the emotions that fit within those umbrellas, so they can identify emotions within themselves, as well as in others.

SAD

DISAPPOINTED

HURT

UNWANTED

GUILTY

ANGRY

ANNOYED

JEALOUS

FRUSTRATED

SCARED

NERVOUS

ANXIOUS

EMBARRASSED

HAPPY

THANKFUL

CONTENT

HOPEFUL

EXCITED

The middle of a blotchy-faced, tear-stained tantrum is not a teachable moment, it's a moment for connection. Once your child feels connected to you, you can redirect behaviour. Daniel Siegel, in *No Drama Discipline*, argues that by being proactive and letting your children connect with you when they're experiencing a tantrum, you may not even need to redirect your child's behaviour – they will do it themselves once they've calmed down. Siegel uses the term 'mindsight': being aware of what is going on below the surface in a situation. It's about understanding behaviour rather than justifying it, and dealing with the reason for the behaviour rather than the behaviour itself.

All of this has to be done with boundaries. Families have rules. In relation to tantrums in our house, the kids can punch pillows or scream, but there is no hitting, no slamming doors and no throwing things. Jack does a 'superchill' where he hugs his body, although his tantrums are fewer and further between these days. Alice is just starting to have those threenager tantrums, and she growls – it is the best noise! I never want them to feel they can't communicate their frustrations, because it is a great strength to be able to identify how you feel.

We learn to regulate as we get older, but we don't learn this if we never get to experience big emotions. So sometimes, let your child go through a big emotion. And if you see another parent whose child is having a big emotion, don't roll your eyes, don't look away. Smile, and if you can, tell them they're doing a good job.

23. Lose things forever

You know Peso, the little penguin from *Octonauts*?
When Jack was two he was OBSESSED with Peso.
He had a little plastic toy Peso that would ride
along the floor. He wanted to take it into day care
so badly. He begged. I said no. He pleaded. I said no.
He was really getting on my nerves, so I said, 'Sure,
but if you lose Peso, he is gone forever.'

'Absolutely, I will not lose Peso.'

We all know how that story ended. And no, I didn't
wander around the day care helping him look for
Peso. I didn't buy him another one. I'd told him
that was the deal, and that was it. This is Nassim
Nicholas Taleb's concept of antifragility in action –

it is upsetting when it happens, but it helps us to
not to make the same mistake again. We grow from
the experience.

There are some genius hacks that parents have
invented over the decades to protect kids from
losing toys – from buying multiples of comforters
(Alice has about seven of those bunnies with the
blanket attached), attaching an elastic to a teddy
so it can be wrapped around your child's wrist (this
is especially helpful when travelling), and of course,
LABELLING EVERYTHING. But let your child learn
that if they take a toy somewhere and there is a
risk of losing it, that risk is real. It will teach them
to appreciate and look after their stuff.

24. Wash the car

I originally had this as a risk for older kids, but as with a lot of skills in life, it really needs to start way before you expect your kids to be able to do it – and before it's going to earn them any pocket money.

Washing the car is not something I am good at, mainly because I am short. Nor is it something I do regularly – I don't mind my car being dirty. But boy, kids add a lot of mess to cars, don't they? I am still shocked that car companies haven't made a product that specifically gets hardened masticated Milk Arrowroot biscuits out of car seats. So all the more reason to get kids involved in cleaning up

the mess they create. They will love getting sudsy and wet (this is probably not one for the middle of winter). And it is also a great opportunity to talk to kids about not wasting water.

Give them one job to do for the whole car wash at first. My daughter at age three spent ten minutes cleaning one hubcap, and it was the shiniest hubcap there ever has been. As your child gets older – and frankly, taller – they can get more involved with the whole car-washing process, until it becomes a job that they can do on their own.

School days

(5–10)

Whether your child has been attending day care or preschool or not, starting 'big school' is a huge jump. I remember Jack was exhausted by Thursdays in his first term at school, and Fridays were always collapse-in-a-heap-on-the-couch nights. But school also opens up the world beyond the family, and there are moments of insight into who your child will be when they grow up. How they navigate the intricacies of the playground and the classroom, and the way they organise themselves will help shape them for life. These risks give you some ideas for how to nurture these skills in a safe and unconditional environment, promoting security and safety.

25. Be socially awkward

As a teacher, I have had a handful of parents ring me to get their child out of detention because the student is sorry/is busy/didn't do it, or – my personal favourite – it was the parent's fault. And I teach *teenagers*. If the parent is stepping in to defend their child at age fifteen or seventeen, you can bet they were doing it beforehand, too. This risks removing a child's ability to develop their own self-advocacy skills.

Socially awkward situations are learning and growing opportunities. When your child is faced with a difficult situation at school, or a disagreement with a friend, talk to them about it. Ask them what they want out of the situation and what consequences they need to face with it. Role-play how they might handle it. Remember that the best outcome of an uncomfortable social situation is that your child learns from it. We need to learn how to deal with all types of people. These sorts of interactions and events shape the person we become.

This does not mean that you should ignore bullying or serious issues that may be occurring. It does mean that when you do step in, it should be because the issue is serious enough to justify you doing so, and because your child has already tried to deal with it on their own.

The worst parenting decision would be to deal with your child's issues in a way that they find embarrassing, because then they won't tell you about them anymore. Instead, build a relationship focused on communication. It's about giving your child the tools they need to deal with these situations, and trusting that they will, and them knowing that they can ask for advice when they need it.

26. Suck at something

We all suck at one thing, at least. Me, I suck at handball. Sometimes when students play it at school they ask me to join in, and honestly, it is embarrassing. Yes yes, I know I should have a growth mindset, but honestly, isn't it okay to just suck at a few things? I'm not prepared to dedicate 10,000 hours to honing my handball skills just so I don't feel like a numpty in front of a bunch of teenagers.

The fact is, in order to develop competencies in students, we need to expose them to activities they may not be competent at. Not all activities will suit all children. That is not a reason to avoid trying them out. This is especially the case if your child is really good at something.

Imagine for a second that your child is excellent at a particular sport and plays it all through school, and then for some reason in Year 11 they don't get into *the team*. That would be shattering; it would be

really hard for your child, and for the whole family. I've seen this happen to many students. Often people find the first rejection the hardest, simply because they've never gone through it. They don't have the resilience or the experience to understand what is happening, let alone be able to respond to it.

Encouraging your child to try activities that they may not be brilliant at – and encouraging them to persevere with those activities – allows for conversations that also develop social emotional learning. It reminds them that there are activities they won't excel at and strengthens the confidence they have in the activities they are competent in. It gives them the experience of knowing what it's like to not have that competence, and the empathy to help mates who are going through moments of rejection. Remember, life is hardest for those who have always had it easy.

27. Show weakness

As a parent, it is common to want to be an unbreakable superhero. And that is understandable – you always want to be the best parent you can be. But it is very difficult to raise children who believe that failure is a normal part of life, if they never see us fail.

I have spoken to parents whose children are going through difficulties – maybe academic, maybe social, it could be anything. The parents usually tell me that they've been through all of these experiences themselves. But if your kids aren't seeing you experience the frustrations of life, they may not believe you when you tell them that mistakes are part of learning, or start espousing growth mindsets and grit.

Even more than that, parenting is hard, and it's okay to admit that sometimes, and to be tired. Parents are juggling more in their lives than ever before – whether it's full-time work, or being a single parent, staying on top of communication from school and day care, or those extracurricular activities that mean the school day never seems to end.

Your children should not be your sounding board after a bad day at home or at work, but a bit of honesty now and then can be helpful. If your child tells you they had a bad day at school, let them know you have bad days too, and that's okay. The first time my six-year-old told me I seemed stressed I was both horrified and proud. I didn't want him to know I was stressed, but I was impressed that he could recognise and identify the emotion. If you give your children the opportunity to see you experiencing your emotions honestly, then they will feel safe in theirs.

28. Play with fire

Even the smallest risks can offer great opportunities to talk about bigger issues. Using a match to light a candle can be a chance to talk about how fire works and why it is dangerous. Our instinct as parents is often to protect kids from these things until we're sure they can handle them – but there's only one way for them to reach that point. Show them how it works.

I have friends who let their kids light candles on any cakes, not just birthday cakes (and of course let the kids blow them out). This is a great way of teaching their kids more about fire risks, and it's also just super fun – plus, it means you are more likely to know where your candles are because you'll be using them more regularly, which is always handy!

29. Wear ugg boots with swimmers

My son had this thing for a while where he liked to wear grey pants and a grey top, or blue pants and a blue top. I have a friend who is a fashion editor, and one day I was telling him how I thought it was really daggy. My friend told me it is called tonal dressing, and it's actually really cool. Who knew? My kid is a fashion icon.

It is always important to give children options and choices. Choices give children power and autonomy, and help them develop a stronger sense of self. Let your children choose their own outfits when it's appropriate, and next time you need to shop for new clothes, let them choose their own. As always,

create boundaries around their choices – 'you need a pair of warm pants, you need a jumper, you can choose up to two T-shirts, it can only cost a certain amount'. But let them have some say in the decisions. Giving your child some choice in the matter will also lead to less arguments over what to wear.

When we are talking about fashion, we also need to talk about gender norms with kids. As the mother of a boy first and a girl second, it drove me insane how the pants you would buy for little girls never had pockets for holding treasures like sticks or leaves or pebbles the way boys' pants do. Or that it can be

impossible to find pyjamas for girls that don't have princesses on them. I never thought I'd be having a philosophical debate with myself on the subject of unicorns, but there I was at Kmart one day trying to decide whether or not they were aligned with trying to raise a feminist. I should at this point mention fashion writer and novelist Maggie Alderson's excellent argument on whether or not to dress young girls in pink. Her theory is that if your child wants to wear five shades of pink, embrace it, lest they rebel by wearing too much chiffon and tutus when they're grown up like Baby Spice or Anna Nicole Smith.

So let your kid choose their own outfits, whether that means leaning into the pink and frilly or the camo and blue. This is where your child's personality comes out. So no, they can't dress as Elsa for every event, but why have that battle on a Saturday morning when you're not going anywhere? And ultimately, by giving your kids a say most of the time, they will hopefully be more flexible when they have to wear the jumper Aunt Nora gave them, just this once, okay?

30. Understand when something goes wrong

Life has risks, plans get cancelled, things go wrong. It is how we deal with these things that defines us – our resilience in really crappy times. It's all well and good to be resilient when everything is going well, it's another when everything turns upside down. In 2020 we saw the whole world stop as everyone retreated into their homes to flatten the curve of the coronavirus. Plans were upended, schools were shut, jobs and lives were lost. Alice, who was only three at the time, did not mind having more time at home, but Jack really felt the loss of his friends, and would often get frustrated with his little sister.

As parents it's natural to want to avoid disappointing your kids by changing plans or by not letting them attend their friend's birthday because you have to go to Great-Aunt Beryl's eightieth instead. But as adults, we often have to do something we don't want to do (go to a five-year-old's birthday party, for example) instead of what we want to do. Ultimately, we have to get kids used to this at some point, right?

So how do you talk to your kids about things going wrong? What can you do? You can keep it in perspective – remind them that there is still love and gratitude in life. You can talk to them about option B: what will you do now that you know you can't go ahead with the original plan? How can you make another plan, one that could be even more fun? When something goes wrong, know that your child is learning how to handle it, and that is preparing them for future experiences.

Life does not always go as planned in bigger ways as well. Parents separate, relatives die, and we feel grief in a whole new sense. Death, like taxes, is a part of life, but is dealt with vastly differently. How we talk about death with children is a very personal choice, but in general the rule of honesty at an age-appropriate level works for almost any difficult conversation.

31. Know that it's okay to have the kid without the thing

Beyblades, Battle Gongs, Pokémon: schoolyards are filled with kids bragging about the stuff they have, and it can lead to your kid thinking that their life is SO UNFAIR and why don't they have the latest superblaster, etc.

It is very easy to think that spending the ten dollars on the toy or getting your kid to earn enough pocket money to buy it is the best way to go, but what if it isn't? Ultimately, life is full of differences, and it can be incredibly unfair. I'm not saying raise your child without any toys, just that you don't

have to give in to every trend. Your kid gets other
things, or does other stuff, or eats other food. Your
kid is loved. Your kid does not need the latest thing,
and maybe not having that thing will give them a
bit more empathy for the kids who don't have the
next thing that sweeps through the playground.

32. Shrink a few socks

I once dated a guy who had never done laundry. He was a fully grown adult. This risk is to ensure you never have that child.

This risk can – and should – start way before age five. When Alice was two, she would put her clothes in the laundry basket when she was getting ready for a bath. Jack, who is not yet eight, carries the laundry basket downstairs and sprays his clothes (and half the laundry) with stain remover. But in terms of managing real risk, don't trust kids with laundry detergent until they are older.

This risk is a great opportunity for chats. Laundry starts together, sitting on the floor sorting clothes. My daughter sits and watches the washing machine spin when we wash her comforters, and then we hang them out together on the line, like the

beautiful Shirley Hughes book *Dogger*. You can get into the big life discussion of whether you try to pair socks before hanging them out or do this once they're dry. You can talk about why hanging clothes to dry is better for the environment. And then you can chat about anything and everything as you fold.

Doing laundry is part of being a member of a family. Okay, yes, by leaving it to the kids, you do risk your whites becoming pink, or a few rogue garments taking some punishment (maybe make this one a calculated risk and set any cashmere aside for the time being), but the gains your child will make in terms of independence and responsibility will far outweigh any sacrificed socks and jocks. It helps everyone, and it means that we can all do a bit less laundry. And that is a win.

33. Negotiate what's for dinner

Everyone does family dinners differently. Some parents work late, so they can't eat dinner with their kids. Others have dinner together every night. Some sit and watch their kids eat bolognese or sausages and veggies, then have their adult dinner together once the kids have gone to bed, perhaps because they can't face another plate of bolognese or sausages and veggies.

Where possible, sharing meals as a family a few times a week is very important for developing connectedness and foundation. But it is also important that not every dinner is about the kids. If you get stuck in the rut of only ever serving what you think your kids will like, then for one thing, you'll get really sick of cooking – or eating – the same

thing, and for another, your kids will never develop their tastebuds. That's where this risk comes in.

Involve your kids in your family meal planning. I don't mean giving them full control and agreeing to cake for dinner, but make them part of the discussion. Teach them to compromise and accommodate everyone's preferences, rather than having you constantly accommodate theirs. This also sets the standard that no, you don't have to like everything you eat, but you do have to try it.

This risk is especially good if it involves takeaway food, because you don't actually have to cook and you can get a bit more adventurous with your choices (no more pizza).

34. Disagree with them

As a teacher, I have given out a lot of consequences –
for not wearing the correct uniform, for not doing
homework, for being rude. Almost every time, and
especially with girls, you hear them reflexively say,
'That is so unfair, X was doing it too.' Dr Justin
Coulson has a great TED talk on rebels: how we love
the idea of them but 'hate the idea of them in our
living rooms'. He talks about the difference between
the eye-rolling, contrary 'reflexive rebels' and
thoughtful 'reflective rebels'. A reflective rebel is one
who thinks before they rebel, or rebels with some
consideration. This risk is about having arguments
with your kids during which you treat them with
respect and receptivity, and help turn them into
reflective rebels.

Arguments, disagreements, debates and banter are part of life. Whether it be in a marriage, at work or with friends, you will disagree with someone at some point. But there are so many ways that disagreements can 'go bad'. You might be too aggressive, or too passive. You might hurl insults or ad hominems at people, you might get too emotional, you might not see the other person's perspective, you might want to storm out.

As parents, we see our children develop from just crying when something doesn't go their way, to saying no, to getting angry, to storming off, to starting to argue, calling names, and refusing to interact. We need to take the risk of teaching them how to argue, and role-model disagreements in a positive way. We need to teach them the art of compromise, and explain that sometimes (okay, most of the time) you do just get to have your say because you are the parent. But we also want to know that our children can question authority respectfully. We never want them to stop asking why, but we also don't want to get a phone call from the principal about having 'the problem child'.

A child who doesn't see any point in arguing because their parents are so authoritarian will believe they have no power to stand up for themselves. The alternative is the child whose parents have given in every time that child has argued. That child is in for one hell of a reality check when they start disagreeing with people who don't love them unconditionally.

I put it to you that there are some things we do as parents that might not nurture our children's ability to argue. Words like 'because I said so' shut down their ability to respond. Saying 'no ifs or buts, just do it' doesn't give them the opportunity to think about what might happen if the situation was different. Now, sometimes it is a 'no ifs or buts' situation and you do just have to 'do as I say because I'm in charge'. But there are other times when there is more time, when there is more space, when you might want to explain to your child WHY you said so, and ask them HOW it could be different. You might want to consider modelling 'I hear you are saying X, but I feel Y'. You could even teach them how to write out their argument explaining how they think something should go. Help them to understand constructive criticism and appreciate that everyone has different points of view.

Learning to disagree and confront problems also helps children learn to develop their own boundaries, and to respect others. At school, there are clear boundaries written down – these are the school rules – but as we grow up, sometimes external boundaries can be harder to recognise unless we have learned how to notice and recognise our own. We want children to know that when they say no it is respected, and that their point of view has been heard, even if it is argued with. This ability to be a reflective rebel, as Dr Coulson argues, means they will have the strength later in life to stand up for their own boundaries when faced with peer pressure.

And if you worry that maybe your child is a little too argumentative, I strongly recommend steering them towards school debating.

35. **Forget to pack undies**

Every day we pack what we need – our wallet and phone, snacks, the clothes we will wear to work after we've been to the gym. We (mostly) get this right because we've had years of practice. Whether it is for school, a sleepover or a holiday, learning to pack is a skill you want your kid to get a handle on sooner rather than later.

On the website Travel Without Tears, author Sally Webb argues that children can be packing their own bags, or at least repacking them, from age three. This risk can start at a very low level of importance – ask your child to choose three toys or three books to take with them that fit into their bag. Then it will be clothing for a trip. It might be good to set some parameters around this, such as what the weather will be like, or whether you are taking suitcases or just backpacks. Involve them in the packing of toiletries but don't depend on them to remember the asthma inhaler and Panadol.

As your child grows up this can become a literacy activity as well – get them to write out a list of the things they want to pack. Talk to them about packing items of clothing that go with other items, or about what shoes you need at the beach.

You can't pack everything on a holiday. This risk teaches children that they need to make choices in life, and every choice has an opportunity cost. Packing ten Beanie Boos means they will, yes, have all their Beanie Boos, but it will also mean they don't have any games or books. And of course sometimes we forget something important, like

undies, but it just makes for a good problem-solving opportunity – and they probably won't forget again!

36. Start conversations with people

Teaching kids how to start conversations is really important for their social development, their resilience (because conversations don't always go as planned), and also for their empathy. You learn to be a nicer person by interacting with others.

Journalist and author Dr Julia Baird once wrote an article about parenting and I clearly remember her saying, 'The rule at our dinner table is that every child must ask every visiting adult two questions, so they learn to think about people around them instead of just batting away cliched questions like: "How is school?"' I have tried to adopt this in our family, and to be honest, the risk is what the heck our children are going to ask. For example, 'Why don't you have any hair?' Or, 'How come your boyfriend doesn't come round anymore?' to a friend who just went through a break-up. Like I said, it's a great opportunity to teach the kids to develop empathy.

Psychologist Dr Judith Locke has a three-question rule: if you have asked your child three questions and they haven't asked you one, stop talking. Allow gaps for them to think about a question they might ask you back, and remind them about two-way conversations.

Teach your child the difference between closed and open-ended questions, and remind them when they've used a closed one by curtly saying yes or no in response. A brilliant junior teacher once told us about the idea of 'ice cream instead of popcorn' in a professional learning session: in a conversation, your comments should be like ice cream, scooped on top of the other person's scoop of conversation, instead of popcorn that randomly pops around the room with no links. I think adults can still struggle with this, and I know sometimes my brain connects totally random ideas and the link is known only to me. But that idea of a multi-scooped ice cream is a great visual for kids to understand.

Make sure your child has things to talk about. It is very hard to have a conversation with someone if they have no content. Encourage their interests wherever you can, share interesting stories and talk to them about things you both like. I have learned about Minecraft so I can talk about that with my kids. There are daily kids' news podcasts, like Squiz Kids, that deliver current affairs in an age-appropriate way so you can listen and discuss them afterwards.

And leave your kids to talk among themselves (or with cousins or friends) as well. If you have ever been at a party with a group of friends and you notice there is one person who is just brilliant at small talk, chances are that person has a lot of siblings.

37. Learn to use a knife 👍💚 without losing a finger

Some skills sound terrifying – the ability to wield sharp instruments is one a lot of parents get caught up over. But using a knife is an important fine motor skill, and how else are you going to get them to do all your kitchen prep? There's really only one way for your kid to learn how to use a knife, and that's ... to use a knife. As with so many things, the earlier you start, the more proficient they'll become. A great way to introduce knife skills is through soap carving. Carving soap with a dinner knife is incredibly cheap, fun, creative, messy (yet squeaky clean) and, yes, a bit risky.

Wait until bulk packs of soap are on sale at the supermarket, and then buy a lot of soap (don't worry, it will all get used). Then, choose a normal knife. Not a plastic kid's one, because that won't do anything, and not a sharpened Japanese sashimi knife, because that would be a waste of a perfectly good knife and a few fingers. Talk to your child about knife safety: show them how to hold a knife, and make sure they know to never cut towards their body.

Next, outline a shape on the soap, and demonstrate to your child how to shave the soap into that shape – again, go away from your body. Then let them try. If your child is one who can focus and wants to make something really pretty, this activity can last for hours.

When your child's excellent fish, shark, vampire, letter, monster, bike or map of Australia is done, collect all the scraps and either make them into nice-smelling soaps for gifts (another skill we have probably all forgotten) or just use them in the bath.

38. Prep them to go solo

This is a bit like doomsday prepping: on one hand, you hope the day will never come, and on the other, you want to be prepared for when it does. For that reason, this is a risk for parents rather than for kids. The thought of your child going out into the big wide world alone may seem terrifying, but one day, it will happen. It might be when they are teenagers, or it could be when they are younger. Maybe it will be planned, or maybe it will just happen – they could get lost in the supermarket, or run through the trees at the park looking for their ball and then suddenly have no idea where you are (hypothetically). Before that day comes, start preparing them.

Ask yourself the following questions.

☑ Does your child know your actual name (not 'Mum' or 'Dad')?

☑ What about your mobile number? Who would they call if they couldn't contact you?

☑ Do they know their address? Is there a local school, shop or landmark from which they could direct someone to your house?

☑ Do they know what to do in case of emergency? Do they know how to call 000?

☑ And the big question: can they identify when they feel unsafe?

Jack and I practised saying where he lived and I showed him how to use a phone. We spent a bit of time learning my mobile number. I thought this would come in really useful if he were ever faced with a scary situation. Instead, a few weeks later I received a text message from a number I didn't recognise saying, 'Hi, our kids are in kindy together and Jack gave me your phone number to arrange a playdate, hope it's the right number.'

So obviously the other risk here is that your role as social secretary will really ramp up.

But the biggest part of solo prepping is talking to your child about how they can know that they feel unsafe. Preschools today are great at teaching kids the 'UNDIES rule' for understanding their own safety around their bodies, which includes getting them to nominate the 'five heroes' who they trust above all others. Beyond these concepts, talk to your child about what it is to feel safe. Stranger danger is still very much a thing, but what if your child was faced with a choice between not talking to any strangers, or asking a stranger to help them call

their parents if they are lost? Which decision would be the best one? Talk to your child about people in the local area they can trust.

When I was growing up there were 'safety houses'. You could see which houses in your neighbourhood had the friendly sticker that showed its residents had had criminal history checks and could be trusted if children needed help. The campaign was discontinued a few years ago, and one of the reasons cited was that kids are driven everywhere now, so it isn't needed anymore. This just shows the cycles that we perpetuate when we don't let kids take some risks.

39. Keep something alive

We used to have two dogs, Spook and Bandit, but when Alice was born we gave them to some friends because they (the dogs, not the friends) were not adjusting well to having two small people usurping them. They communicated their displeasure by urinating on the kids' toys. With two full-time jobs we just couldn't do two kids and two dogs, and frankly, giving the kids away seemed like an overreaction.

Now Jack is at school though, I do think of how growing up, my family had a dog, Rusty. My brother and I would walk Rusty, feed him, and he would sit on our feet while we watched TV and get right up in our face before letting out a massive fart. My parents, being the lawyers they were, had my brother (aged seven) sign a contract of dog ownership, which listed the jobs he had to do.

(That was slightly futile because it didn't include a subsection on what happens if the child goes overseas at age eighteen.)

There is something to be said for keeping a pet alive. It teaches kids about responsibility, companionship (sure, maybe not with a hermit crab), and empathy. Depending on the kind of pet that suits your family, pets can bring risks as well, from health issues (the pet's) to sanity issues (yours, from the mess). Of course, with life comes death, and having a pet will at some point mean your family will mourn and talk about death, as discussed in risk 30.

Studies have shown that pets give children a greater sense of self-esteem and security during stressful times. So pet ownership for children can offer great opportunities for increased responsibility, autonomy and social benefits. If you can't justify getting a dog – and I really don't suggest it unless the whole family wants one – maybe a fish or a plant is a less intensive way to introduce this idea. We agreed Jack could get a pet fish to keep alive for a while before there is any discussion about getting another dog.

40. Go alone

In 2018 the Australian Heart Foundation conducted a survey that looked into children walking or riding to school. The results paint a picture of risk avoidance, which in turn increases risk for later life. The survey showed that only 15–20 per cent of children walk or ride their bikes to school. The main reasons given for driving kids were safety and time. Ironically, most parents said they were concerned the traffic was too busy to let their kids walk – their cars are contributing to that traffic. Parents were also worried not about authorities but about 'local mums' or 'concerned citizens' who would judge them for letting their kid ride to school.

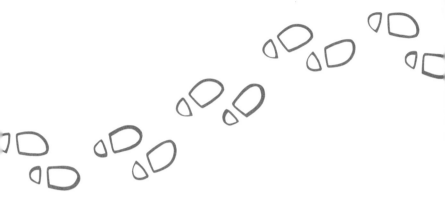

Across the world there are very different parenting moments happening. In Japan, children are encouraged to leave the house and run errands on their own from the age of two or three. There is even a TV show called *Hajimete no Otsukai* or 'My First Errand'. In Switzerland over 75 per cent of children walk to and from school. On the first day of kindergarten, Swiss children are given a reflective necklace to make them extra visible to cars. They have to wear the necklace for two years, until they start big school when they're six. By contrast, in Vermont, USA, in 2011, Kim Brooks left her son in the car (with the windows down) for five minutes to get him some headphones for a plane trip. Within a few days she had been contacted by the police for breaking the law.

In both Japan and Switzerland, there is an onus on the bystander to step in and help the child if needed. In America, and to a similar extent in Australia, it can feel as though you are parenting in an Orwellian state. Japan has a very low crime rate, but Australia's actually isn't much higher. However, we just don't have that expectation of others in Australia. In fact, we are more in fear of judgement from bystanders than we are of the police getting involved.

Letting your children go to school (or the shops or a friend's house) alone is a complex risk, especially because the laws in relation to child safety and children being on their own at home or in public can be bloody hard to figure out. Especially if you are not a lawyer. Your kid's sense of responsibility, your local community, and whether there are places for your kid to walk to are all going to be major factors in this decision. As a caveat, I will add here that Jack is not yet eight, and he has been allowed to walk some distances on his own. Sometimes on the way home he will take a different way and I will meet him at the next corner, or he'll go bike riding

down the laneways and I can't see him for all of 150 metres as he turns a corner.

But I think this is a really important risk that can be safe and appropriate for children under the age of ten, depending on the kid and the context. Some families have limited options when it comes to school transport – especially children in regional areas or without access to good public transport. But in my years working in schools, I have seen children being driven less than two kilometres to and from school, and can't help but feel that getting to school on their own is a risk children would seriously benefit from undertaking themselves. Fifteen minutes of riding or walking twice a day would get children halfway to the one hour of daily exercise that is recommended for school-aged children.

One factor to be considered is the age of siblings. You might be fine with your ten-year-old walking to school with a six-year-old, but in two years' time when the then-twelve-year-old changes school, is it okay for the eight-year-old to walk on their own? That's up to you. There are issues involving a child's peripheral vision that need to be considered – studies have shown that seven-year-olds have weaker peripheral vision than ten- or eleven-year-olds. The child's ability to identify vehicles and understand their own visibility are also still developing at this age.

The best answer to all of this, of course, is role-modelling safe pedestrian behaviour, and explaining how to be a responsible pedestrian from as early as you can. My kids know to stop at the corner of the road, and if I've got shopping bags in one hand and I'm holding Alice's in the other, Jack will sometimes cross the road on his own. I always tell them both to cross the road 'with intent', because the worst thing a kid can do is dawdle.

41. Get the bus

Letting her ten-year-old get public transport earned Lenore Skenazy the title of 'worst mother in the world', but she did it because her kid loved getting the subway and reading maps, and she knew he was old enough to do it.

Once you have solo prepped your child, and they have done some small errands on their own, maybe it's time to get them on public transport. School students are often eligible for free or heavily discounted transport, and getting your child comfortable with public transport means you are less likely to become a taxi driver later in life.

There are many different ways you can start this risk – maybe you get the bus with your child but don't sit with them. Or you could put them on a short bus ride – say, to three or four stops away – and meet them there. Don't do it in peak hour, and let the bus driver know what you are doing – or let your child know what they should say in response to any questions. Make sure they are comfortable with getting buses in general, and with that bus route in particular. Then eventually, let your child take public transport to wherever the family is going one day, and meet them there.

42. Take charge of the kitchen

My Year 11 English teacher said that everyone should have seven meals they can make without a recipe. To be honest, at that point I don't think I had any. I think the peak of my cooking ability was the year before we had kids. Since then I have been so consistently beaten by fussy eating and general kid dinner chaos that I haven't done much cooking for the fun of it.

What recipes do you want your kid to be able to make by the time they are teenagers? I recommend introducing them to a new recipe every few months so they can build up their repertoire. Get them involved in choosing what to have for dinner and finding a recipe. You could watch *Junior MasterChef* and *Nailed It!* for inspiration, or find a cookbook you both enjoy. Or you can just start with what they like eating. Sure, your meals might be a bit hit and miss for a while, but the payoff will be worth it. Imagine not having to cook dinner. Every. Single. Night.

Teach your kids a bit about supply chain logistics. Work with them on writing the shopping list, explaining concepts like budgets and food waste (if you buy a whole bag of onions, what are you going to do with the other seven of them?). Have them read the recipe and start by cooking it with them, helping them with safe knife skills and food preparation, then eventually work yourself out of the process. May I suggest a glass of wine while they cook? You can be management and quality control. Once they've mastered that recipe, start on another one.

Make it enjoyable, of course, but also remember that in reality, not everyone is a MasterChef. Cooking isn't always going to be fun – sometimes you just have to put a meal together.

43. Be the first risky parent

It is difficult to be the first parent to be a bit 'risky' in a family, or a group of friends, or a school. You might be the subject of 'looks' when letting the kids ride their skateboards, or struggle on the play equipment that one minute longer than other parents would. But don't let that stop you.

Remind yourself why you are taking risks with your kids. It is so they develop skills like resilience, resourcefulness and empathy, and so they generally grow up to be better humans. It is not for external validation from other parents or from grandparents.

Secondly, talk to local community leaders about it. If your kid is at school already, talk to the school principal or P&C and ask for definitive answers on questions like what age kids are allowed to walk to and from school. Find out what your local police think of kids riding bikes on the footpath. If your child is going to walk to a local shop to buy milk, maybe let the shopkeeper know, so they don't freak out.

Thirdly, build a bit of an army of other pro-risk mums or dads. I definitely suggest buying many copies of this book for friends! Start in your neighbourhood – no kid wants to go bike riding after school alone. One way that conversations around risk can start is when other parents comment that your kid is allowed to do things that their kids may not be able to, or allowed to. Without being annoying about it, explain how you're trying to raise them to be self-motivated and resilient. Or hark back to your own childhood, when you were able to do these things, and point out that the world is actually safer now than it was when you were kids.

44. Say thank you

How awesome is receiving a thank-you note? Like an actual hand-written letter, with a stamp on it. Writing thank-you notes is a skill we need to teach our kids. Okay, gratitude isn't really a risk, but a lack of gratitude is. Entitlement is a risk. A dependent mentality is a risk. And gratitude can be instilled earlier than you think.

The benefits of gratitude have been extensively discussed and researched and TED-talked about. People who regularly practise gratitude are healthier and happier. This isn't limited to writing thank-you notes, of course. Gratitude can – and should – be practised in all sorts of ways. Writing down three good things that happened (or even better, three people who helped you) in a day promotes higher rates of psychological and physical health, to the extent that people who practise gratitude have less aches and pains. Some studies have shown that gratitude even improves sleep – people who spend fifteen minutes before bed writing down what they are grateful for are more likely to sleep better.

Gratitude is great for relationships, both new and old. Noticing and appreciating how others make your life better will, in fact, make your life better. Gratitude makes you more empathetic – when you recognise how people help you, you are more likely to recognise other emotions in people. This also helps boost your own self-esteem, because it means you are more likely to appreciate the way others help you, rather than being resentful of your need for help, which can make you feel devalued.

But gratitude is fundamentally countercultural at the moment. Professor Brené Brown talks about gratitude being vulnerability. Gratitude tears apart the idea that we are absolutely independent and self-sufficient. Being grateful means you see, recognise and admit that other people help you. That we are in relation with other people, and that we cannot do things on our own. For this reason you can't teach your children gratitude while overusing the vertical pronoun in your own life: 'I am so awesome, I did this all by myself, nobody ever helps me with anything'.

Gratitude should be a big part of parenting. You are doing a lot for your child, but as they grow older (and more independent) and you 'do' less for them, gratitude keeps a relationship strong. Raising kids with gratitude and not a sense of owing each other (which promotes shame) develops a healthier, more mature relationship with your children as they grow older. I see this in the students I teach: those who really appreciate their parents and what they do for them, versus those who just expect it.

Apart from writing thank-you notes, there are many other small ways to practise gratitude with your kids. For starters, just say thank you more often – and authentically – and make sure they see you saying it. You'll know you're doing it right if 'thank you' comes naturally and doesn't need to be prompted.

At dinner or family meals, ask questions about each person's day. A colleague once said her family asked three questions: 'What was a good thing that happened in your day? Who did you help? Who did you laugh with?'

Have conversations that develop a sense of appreciation for what happens without us noticing it in society – for example, clean streets are thanks to local councils. Gratitude for farmers who grow food we eat. Gratitude for lifesavers and firefighters. This also works in the home, by noticing how each member of the family contributes.

Finally, help your kids develop an appreciation for what they have, and realistic expectations of what they should have. Avoid the accumulation of crap, and stuff they don't appreciate, and develop a sense of charity. One friend has a 'one toy in, one toy donated' rule, which helps with both gratitude and clutter.

45. Be on the team

If you baulked at your under-five-year-old climbing trees, it is important to note that just 2 per cent of tree climbers have actually broken a bone, whereas 4.3 per cent of children under eighteen who entered an emergency department were there due to sporting injuries. Sport can be dangerous, but it is also incredibly valuable for children.

There is a lot of research on getting kids moving, especially for those who are reluctant to participate at all, and a lot on the effects of focusing on just one particular sport, usually an elite sport. But what about those kids in the middle, not the elite kids, nor the kids who are carried kicking and screaming over their parents' shoulders to each training session? Most kids will be in the centre of the bell curve.

Sport is great exercise, it develops team building and communication skills, and it gives children practical ways to develop resilience. It also teaches kids responsibility. You know all that. But studies have shown that specialising in one sport at a young age increases the risk of overuse injuries (nasty ones). It also increases the pressure associated with playing sport, and can lead to children rejecting that sport entirely. Some research has suggested children shouldn't do more hours of training a week than they are years old – nine hours of training a week sounds like a lot for a nine-year-old.

Developing team skills and being able to understand the benefits of shared responsibility will help serve them later in life. Once when I was teaching, there was a semi-final netball game for a middle-ranking team, and more than half the team didn't turn up to the game because some pop star put on a concert that night. I remember the school's head girl gave the most amazing speech reminding students of their responsibilities to their teams, and saying that if they can't make a game, the worst thing they can do is just not turn up. There are times when your child won't be able to make a practice or a game, and while the goal should always be to get there, the second-best thing is telling your team mates up front if you can't, and taking responsibility for it.

'Being on the team' doesn't just count for sport – the same ideas still apply to being part of the drama troupe, school band or chess squad.

Team activities are also opportunities to consider how involved you want to be as a parent. Dr Judith Locke advises against having both parents and both sets of grandparents at every football game or recital night, because it sets up a very child-focused view of their world. You can't make every game, you have to take it in turns, or you're a single parent. There will be carpools. Remember, the expectation management around this starts developing earlier than you realise. And when you are there to watch, remember you're not there to commentate or to coach (unless you are the coach). Just enjoy it, and that will help your child to enjoy it too.

46. Sleep outside

Look, I'm not exactly a fan of camping, but it is one of those things we do 'for fun' to 'build character', so I had to include it. Despite not loving tents and sleeping-bags, I did enter a career where five days away camping with a dozen fourteen-year-olds was part of the job description, so my choice of work knew camping had something to teach me.

Alice is desperate to go camping – I blame the camping episode of *Bluey*. While she hasn't braved the great outdoors yet, James and Jack have on a few occasions and have loved it. In his book

Camping with Kids, camping afficionado Simon McGrath writes that 'camping encourages us to slow down, to stop and connect with the natural environment around us … It enables us to watch our children play as they make their own discoveries.'

So, risk the dirt, and the discomfort – it'll be worth it. Start in the backyard. As your kids get older you won't even need to camp with them (as you may have gathered, camping is really not my thing). Then, if camping *is* your thing, you could start to go on some adventures together as a family.

Camping is an activity that can be divided between parents, and one that allows for some one-on-one time with parents and kids. It also offers screen-free time, and gives kids a new understanding of slowing down and relaxing. Kids will love the other risks that go alongside camping, like exploring, going to the toilet in the dark (with or without the bunny nightlight) and, of course, building a campfire and having those campfire conversations.

47. Prick a finger

I am an obsessive crocheter and knitter. When people see me crochet, they often ask who taught me. The answer is my grandma Joanna and my friend Julie, and I am very grateful to both of them. But as I yarn over and hook and stitch, I often think that their question is greater than that – it goes to the lost skills we are no longer teaching our children. This risk is about craft, but you could substitute any other skills you learnt as a kid that it may not have occurred to you to teach your children. Or maybe even a skill your parents had that they didn't teach you (YouTube is very helpful for this).

Crafts are risky because you can stuff them up, you can make mistakes and have to redo the whole thing, you can realise you've lost hours of time with nothing to show for it. You can get frustrated and then get better. Craft represents life in general, and practising it helps prepare you for those moments of frustration that we all go through.

Another reason to teach your child a craft, and it can be any craft, is that crafts are good for your wellbeing. There is a sense of flow that occurs, which has a meditative effect. Your brain relaxes, you get challenged and frustrated, you gain a sense of achievement. In other words, it is a great way to practise grit and a growth mindset on a daily basis.

And even if you're not a keen crafter, there are some basic 'craft' skills that are important to have. Much like learning to use a knife, learning to sew on a button, hem clothes or attach a label are all skills that you don't want your kid to find themselves lacking as adults. And if your kid is five, you have thirteen years of school labels ahead of you. Why not get them to do it?

48. Plan a holiday as a family

There is a *lot* of planning that goes into a family holiday, but in the end it needs to be a holiday for everyone, so why shouldn't everyone be involved in that planning? This is risky because it is going to involve a lot of discussing and explaining with children, but now that they've learned how to argue (see risk 34), at least you know the discussions will happen respectfully. Set parameters on a holiday plan – for example, distance from home, budget, maybe a list of no-go places (the Democratic People's Republic of Korea *sounds* like a really friendly place, what with democracy, people and it being a republic, but maybe skip it for now).

Give your kids a chance to think about what they want out of a holiday. Don't shy away from talking to your children about the cost of travel, and why it is something the family chooses to invest in. Talk about what kind of activities they might want to do (swim or play with other kids, for example) and the kinds of activities you want to do (go on hikes or drink cocktails, for example). This will help your kids understand everyone's different perspectives, and also link to the effort involved in organising a holiday, which should help with gratitude, without guilt.

49. Raise a child with boundaries

In risk 34, I mentioned the role of reflective rebels, those who think about what is going on before acting. Teenagers who stop for a second to think about whether it is actually a good idea to ride down a hill in a Coles trolley. Those who question you when you tell them to do something 'because I said so'.

The thing with reflective rebels is that they have started developing boundaries and are learning to use them. Some of us adults have never really developed our own boundaries, and so we end up saying yes to everything. But as parents, we should

have boundaries, and it is really important that we are explicit with both ourselves and our children about what they are. Professor Brené Brown talks about the issue of crossing boundaries or limits when role-modelling to children. If you say no more ice cream, then give them more ice cream anyway, your child will grow up thinking that limits can be broken. This can be bloody exhausting as a parent. Sometimes you do just want to give them another ice cream or ten more minutes of screen time, but going back on your word, changing your limits and letting children push your boundaries shows them that those boundaries don't need to be respected.

As your child grows up, and especially as they approach the teen years, it is important to give them age-appropriate responsibilities, and consequences, and stick to them. Again, this can be exhausting. It is sometimes easier to clean out their lunch box for them than it is to ask them fifteen times to do it. But this is about the development of autonomy and responsibility, and the meaningfulness of that responsibility. If it is their job to clean up after dinner, and they don't but it's cleaned up anyway, then what is the point of them having that job? By raising them with actual boundaries in place, they develop, as self-help author Dr Henry Cloud writes, 'a deep sense of personal responsibility for their own lives'.

This whole 'boundaries' thing is going to lead to a LOT of arguments, especially when your child is at school and spending time at other kids' houses. Your parenting is going to be different to other parents'. For example, I use the screen time function on Jack's iPad, while other parents don't. I'm not judging. The fact is, I am no better a parent than those who don't use screen time. I just do it so I don't have to ask myself how much time he's spent playing Minecraft – I know exactly when he's clocked thirty minutes. And hand on heart, I extend screen time a lot after he's done a chore or a job or spent some time reading. Jack whinges about it: 'Other kids don't have screen time, why do I have to do it? It's unfair.' But I have to be confident in the rules we set. I have to be able to argue my own boundaries and explain to Jack why he has different rules.

Ultimately, it isn't the rules that matter, it isn't how much time they get to spend playing Minecraft – it is that kids need to see you parenting with boundaries. As a result, they learn to respect those boundaries, and they develop their own boundaries and critical-thinking skills. That means maybe they'll stop for a second, and ask themselves whether it is a good idea to ride a trolley down a hill. Maybe they'll still do it, but at least they stopped and thought about it. And maybe they won't do it the next time.

50. Talk about risk

While I don't imagine anyone has worked through this list of risks and ticked them off one by one, there is one risk that I think it's important to finish on. If you are the kind of reader who flicks to the last few pages, this could actually be a good way to start as well!

The language of risk in our society is very negative. I hope that by reading this book, your relationship with risk has developed to help you think about working with risk and managing it, rather than avoiding it altogether. If you are not letting your child be exposed to risks and you are not talking to them about risk, they can't mature enough to assess risks and will continue to be anxious about them. Allowing children to be exposed to risky play that challenges them means they develop that skill, but we also need to change the language around risk.

Risk needs to be discussed openly. If your child wants to do something, talk about what the consequences could be, discuss the chance of something bad happening, and consider what they would do if something did happen.

There is a concept in positive psychology known as active constructive responding. When someone tells us something, we generally have one of four responses, which can be shown on a matrix.

	ACTIVE	PASSIVE
CONSTRUCTIVE	AUTHENTIC, ENTHUSIASTIC SUPPORT	QUIET, DELAYED RESPONSE
DESTRUCTIVE	DEMEANING AND DISMISSING	AVOIDING OR IGNORING

As a parent it is very easy to jump into protective mode and think about everything that could go wrong when your child wants to take a risk. Just say your nine-year-old comes in and says they have been invited to go surfing with another family from school. An active destructive response would be to say, 'Oh, I thought you hated the ocean,' or, 'But what if you hurt yourself?' This is the worst response in relation to risk, because you encourage the idea that the existence of risk is a reason NOT to do something. A passive destructive response would be to decide that they shouldn't go, but instead effectively ignore them. 'Right, well, it's time to get ready for dinner.' A passive constructive response would be to not really respond at all – something like, 'Hmm, we can talk about that later.' This still discourages the child from taking the action.

Instead, you want to use an active constructive response that asks for more information authentically, and engage your child in a discussion about the action before you make any decisions. A rule of thumb is to ask three questions: 'Oh, where do they go surfing? What would you need to bring?

Who else is going?' Being positive as a first instinct develops the conversation and means it will continue and grow. It doesn't mean that you won't discuss the risks eventually, or decide they can't go, it just means that the idea won't be quashed immediately by putting the risks front and centre.

One great activity is 'putting it in perspective'. The University of Pennsylvania's School of Positive Psychology suggests asking what the WORST thing that could happen is (which is often our default), then what the BEST thing that could happen is, and finally, what the most likely outcome is. If you know what you would do in all three situations, then you're less likely to go hell for leather into a stupid decision – and if you do, at least you know what the consequence will be.

As your child moves into the early adolescent years, the noun 'risk' will be replaced by the adjective 'risky'. Teens are risky, and that is always seen as a bad thing. There are a lot of neurological reasons for this, as well as social and emotional causes. As we grow up, our brains start to scan all the potential outcomes of a decision and weigh them up in a more logical way. We recognise the context around facts, and work with that context. Teenagers are still developing that skill. (Dr Dan Siegel's book *Brainstorm* goes into great detail about the effects of dopamine and the teenage brain.) Developing the language of risk and consequence and managing risk effectively might help your teen navigate these decisions. If you can develop your child's self-awareness so they can be a reflective rebel, they will pause for a moment to think about the consequences of actions, and can really consider the pros and cons. This means they will have more of a toolkit for understanding the potential consequences of a risk.

So talk to your child honestly, not only about the possible outcomes of a risk but also about how they need to be weighed up. Let them know that if they can't do it, they can talk to you about it. When it comes to risk-taking, the greatest protective factor you can give your child is a trusting and connected relationship with them, one where they understand the physical, emotional and relational risks that are around, and know that they are loved and supported enough to make their own decisions.

Resources

A list of useful books that helped me write this book and helped me be a parent, and will hopefully help you too:

Baird, Julia, *Phosphorescence: On awe, wonder and things that sustain you when the world goes dark*, HarperCollins Australia (2020)

Barker, Robin, *Baby Love: Everything you need to know about your baby*, Macmillan Publishers Australia (2005)

Brooks, Kim, *Small Animals: Parenthood in the age of fear*, Flatiron Books (2018)

Brooks, Robert, & Goldstein, Sam, *Raising Resilient Children: Fostering strength, hope, and optimism in your child*, McGraw Hill Professional (2002)

Brown, Brené, *The Gifts of Imperfection: Let go of who you think you're supposed to be and embrace who you are*, Hazelden Publishing (2010)

Cooke, Kaz, *Kid-wrangling: The real guide to caring for babies, toddlers and preschoolers*, Viking (2004)

Crabb, Annabel, *The Wife Drought Why women need wives, and men need lives*, Random House Australia (2015)

Erikson, Erik H, *Identity and the Life Cycle*, W W Norton & Company (1994)

Gilbert, Jack, & Knight, Rob, *Dirt Is Good: The advantage of germs for your child's developing immune system*, St. Martin's Press (2017)

Ginsburg, Kenneth R, Ginsburg, Ilana, & Ginsburg, Talia, *Raising Kids to Thrive: Balancing love with expectations and protection with trust*, American Academy of Pediatrics (2015)

Haidt, Jonathan & Lukianoff, Greg, *The Coddling of the American Mind: How good intentions and bad ideas are setting up a generation for failure*, Penguin, UK (2018)

Locke, Judith, *The Bonsai Child: Why modern parenting limits children's potential and practical strategies to turn it around*, Confident and Capable (2015)

Siegel, Daniel J & Bryson, Tina P, *No-drama Discipline: The whole-brain way to calm the chaos and nurture your child's developing mind*, Scribe Publications (2014)

Skenazy, Lenore, *Free-range Kids: How to raise safe, self-reliant children (without going nuts with worry)*, John Wiley & Sons (2009)

Taleb, Nicholas N, *Antifragile: Things that gain from disorder*, Penguin UK (2012)

Waters, Lea, *The Strength Switch: How the new science of strength-based parenting helps your child and your teen flourish*, Scribe Publications (2017)

And some articles and reports, if you want to read a little deeper:

Arnsten, Amy, Mazure, Carolyn & Sinha, Rajita, 'This is your brain in meltdown', *Scientific American*, 306(4), 48–53

Bauer, Ethan, 'Risk vs. reward: Should parents gamble on their kid being the next LeBron James?', *Deseret News*, 20 October 2019

Colin, Chris, 'What is "forest bathing" – and can it make you healthier?', *The Guardian*, 7 October 2019

David, SS, Foot, HC, Chapman, AJ, & Sheehy, NP, 'Peripheral vision and the aetiology of child pedestrian accidents', *British Journal of Psychology*, 77(1), 117–135

Deci, Edward L, & Ryan, Richard M, *Handbook of self-determination research*, University Rochester Press (2004)

Dent, Maggie, 'Parental as anything' podcast, ABC (Australian Broadcasting Corporation), 17 March 2020

Ducharme, Jamie, 'Being bored can be good for you—if you do it right. Here's how', *Time*, 4 January 2019

Department of Education and Training Victoria, 'Travelling to school'

Developing Minds, 'The underwear rule – Seven sentences to use to help keep kids safe from sexual abuse', 25 November 2015

Fredrickson, Barbara L, 'The broaden-and-build theory of positive emotions', *Philosophical transactions of the Royal Society of London, Series B, Biological sciences*, 2004, 359(1449), 1367–1378

Gray, Peter, 'Toddlers want to help and we should let them', *Psychology Today*, 25 September 2018

Green, Adrian M, 'Gratitude', *Greater Good*, 18 June 2020

Gull, Carla, Goldstein, Suzanne L & Rosengarten, T, 'Benefits and risks of tree climbing on child development and resiliency', *International Journal of Early Childhood Environmental Education*, 2017, 5(2), 10

Hesselmar, Bill, Sjoberg, Fei, Saalman, Robert, Aberg, Nils, Adlerberth, Ingegerd & Wold, Agnes E, 'Pacifier cleaning practices and risk of allergy development', *Pediatrics*, 2013, 131(6), e1829–e1837

Acknowledgements

This book, and my entire life, would never have been possible without the love and support of my family. My parents, Malcolm and Lucy, raised my brother, Alex, and I in the mid 80s, and it was in that context that I learned what sensible parenting was. They have always raised us to be curious and kind, to be grateful and charitable. When I became a parent, they offered wisdom and humour when I could find none amid the sleepless nights and anxious days. Mum approached the role of grandmother with her sleeves rolled up and ready to indulge, and has been a pillar of strength and love. And when Dad talks to children, especially to his grandchildren, he always addresses them as the people he knows they will be, with dignity and logic.

My brother, Alex, his wife, Yvonne, and their children, Isla and Ronan, have been overseas for much of this process, but I am always thankful for the moments the kids can share together, playing together in person or on Zoom.

James is the best father a child could ask for, one of excitement and games, footy and fancy dress, challenging discussions, and the ability to find his army officer voice when needed, especially if it involves getting kids to put shoes on. Thank you for your encouragement during this writing process.

It takes a village to raise a family and my village is great. From day one, Sunita and Kerry have been a source of checking in, comparing notes, and luxe plate exchanges. Maureen and Todd have been on the same journey as James and I, and though our distances have been great, they constantly provide love and support. Maria O'Brien welcomed me into the Working Mother's Club and renews the reasons for my membership every day. Andrew knows every way to sneak in vegetables. The community at St Luke's, who welcomed the kids and I with open hearts and have nurtured a love of God in me, while also providing excellent parenting and life advice. The teachers at Jack and Alice's schools, who inspire curiosity and kindness in the kids. The team at wolf, who were our home away from home at stupid o'clock and provided coffee, love, and good chats. The babysitters, Jack whisperers and general people of awesomeness. Linda and Kaye – the greatest friends/aunts/surfing lesbian duo that a girl could ask for. Felicity, Bec, Emily, Helena, Pauline, Mariele, Georgia, Indivi and the entire harem. Thank you for everything.

I have to thank the friends who have held my hand through epic bouts of imposter syndrome, who dispensed wisdom via WhatsApp and who went for walks and coffees and made me laugh through the insanity of parenting. My best friends, Melissa Chan – who is always a sounding board, a fact checker of my life and provider of truth, wisdom and goodness – and Maria Wang-Faulkner – who while in the trenches of lockdown with a two-year-old and a newborn, read this entire manuscript and commented on it. Amelia and JT, who provide laughter, pep talks, and excellent music recommendations. Andrew and Lou, for love and pastries. Sally has been like a sister to me for longer than either of us dare quantify; she is now Aunty Sal to the kids and has lost a mock trial with Jack on at least one occasion. Thank you for helping, and for always being correct. Meersy has been a great friend and a reminder of life beyond parenting; thank you for phone chats on the way home from Lifeline. Thank you Bevan for stylistic advice and WhatsApp chats at all hours. Kumi has been not only a Twitter-turned-IRL friend, but a great support over the past year when life has been complicated, and a firm believer in trusting your gut. Thank you to Leigh, who provides truth bombs like no other. To Mel, who drove up as soon as lockdown lifted to spend quality time together. To Kirstin, Jess and Bec, thank you for your friendship and advice. Thank you to Risé.

Throughout this journey I have constantly had the support and friendship of some wonderful mums at work, especially Bec Herbert, Jo Graffen and Kylie McCullah. I could not have written this book without their friendship and experiences, and I look forward to holiday adventures again soon. My colleagues at St Catherine's are able to make the most frustrating day worthy of tears of laughter, and multiply the joy that comes from a student's success tenfold. Our 'human' leader Beatriz Cartlidge plopped me into a history classroom when I was just a baby teacher, and I am constantly amazed at her ability to tell stories that engage. I acknowledge the wonderful contributions of Elyse Read, the best work wife in the world, not just to editing this book but also to my life. Kylie Wilson has been a wonderful friend and mentor in teaching students about religion, and provider of great laughs. Julie Townsend has been the most inspiring leader at St Catherine's, as she has lived through raising kids and working full time. When Alice was six weeks old she promoted me to Director of Positive Psychology, showing her firm belief that working mothers can do anything (when I did not believe that of myself), and started me on this journey of positive psychology, wellbeing and resilience. In this role I have also been incredibly lucky to work with Deb Clancy, the most no-nonsense yet generous boss I've had. She puts huge faith in those she leads and I am incredibly grateful for her strength and support. Thank you to Sonya, who somehow manages to know everything that is happening at all times across a school of over 1000 students.

The team at Hardie Grant got to know me when I was giving the history teacher's essay-marking treatment on another book they published recently. Arwen Summers and I started a conversation about resilience, and what started as a joke list of ideas became this book, which it would not have been without her stewardship. Arwen, being truly passionate about her work, decided to have a baby during the process in order to truly test out each risk, and I started working with Emily Hart, who has been a wonderful editor. We have worked on this book across different states, during lockdowns, and managed to see eye to eye on almost everything, especially musicals. Vanessa Lanaway has been a brilliant copy editor. And thank you to Sinéad Murphy, who I have also never met, but who has illustrated and designed this book to match the personality of the author and the message perfectly.

Thank you also to the friends and colleagues who read this book over lockdown and provided feedback: Fiona Martin, Annabel Crabb, Lenore Skezany, Ian Hickie, Madonna King, and of course Judith Locke for her wonderful foreword.

This book is about children, and there are some very important children I want to thank. My godchildren, Edward, Charlie, and Betty-Rose John-O'Brien; Max and Georgina Krugman; and Winston Howard. You all have brilliant parents who will raise you to be excellent humans, but know that I am here, at the end of a phone, or in a playground with a babycino, or on a church pew, whenever you want to talk. As your godmother I should probably quote Colossians 3:20 and tell you to obey your parents in everything, but instead I think I will remind you to be kind to one another, tenderhearted and forgiving.

And finally, to the two children who made me a mother, make me smile every day, challenge my mind and broaden my heart. Jack and Alice, you are the greatest loves of my life. You are growing into people of strength and integrity, of kindness and empathy, of curiosity and thought. Jack, at seven you are able to understand how other people feel with more emotional intelligence than most adults have. Hold on to that, it is such a strength. Alice, you are so strong and determined and I hope you never let anyone or anything make you want to be less than that. I look forward to taking these risks with you, and watching you grow into kind, generous and resilient people.

Published in 2021 by Hardie Grant Books,
an imprint of Hardie Grant Publishing

Hardie Grant Books (Melbourne)
Building 1, 658 Church Street
Richmond, Victoria 3121

Hardie Grant Books (London)
5th & 6th Floors
52–54 Southwark Street
London SE1 1UN

hardiegrantbooks.com

Hardie Grant acknowledges the Traditional Owners of the country on which we work, the Wurundjeri people of the Kulin nation and the Gadigal people of the Eora nation, and recognises their continuing connection to the land, waters and culture. We pay our respects to their Elders past, present and emerging.

A catalogue record for this
book is available from the
NATIONAL LIBRARY OF AUSTRALIA — National Library of Australia

50 Risks to Take With Your Kids
ISBN 9781 74379 634 4

10 9 8 7 6 5 4 3 2 1

Colour reproduction by Splitting Image Colour Studio
Printed in China by Leo Paper Products LTD.

FSC
www.fsc.org
MIX
Paper from
responsible sources
FSC® C020056

The paper this book is printed on is from FSC®-certified forests and other sources. FSC® promotes environmentally responsible, socially beneficial and economically viable management of the world's forests.